The
Essential Guide to
D   ~on

HOW TO AVOID DANGEROUS SITUATIONS, OVERPOWERING INDIVIDUALS AND DATE RAPE

Scott Lindquist
F.C.P.P., C.P.S., Florida Crime Prevention Practitioner and Crime Prevention Specialist

SOURCEBOOKS, INC.
NAPERVILLE, ILLINOIS

Published by Sourcebooks, Inc.
P.O. Box 4410
Naperville, IL 60567-4410
630-961-3900
Fax: 630-961-2168

Originally published in 1999. This is a revised edition.

Library of Congress Cataloging-in-Publication Data

Lindquist, Scott.
  The essential guide to date rape prevention : how to avoid dangerous situations, overpowering individuals and date rape / Scott Lindquist. -- Rev. ed.
      p. cm.
  Rev. ed. of: The date rape prevention book. 2000.
  Includes bibliographical references and index.
  ISBN-13: 978-1-4022-1022-8
  ISBN-10: 1-4022-1022-1
  1. Date rape--United States. 2. Date rape--United States--Prevention. I. Lindquist, Scott. Date rape prevention book. II. Title.

HV6561.L56 2007
613.6'63--dc22

                                    2007026519

                Printed and bound in the United States of America
                    VP 10 9 8 7 6 5 4 3 2

Dedicated to Rev. Sydney A. Magill-Lindquist

This book is dedicated to my wife Sydney.
Her constant love and undying support for me and this work is
a testament, not only to her faith in me, but also to her conviction that all
women have the right to be safe and free from fear, intimidation,
and control. I can only wish that all men might have the good fortune
and blessing of a partner who has always been in my corner,
even when I wasn't.

Thank you to all those who have made this book possible.

Deborah Werksman, my editor, has been influential in guiding my hand to be clear and simple in my communication. She has taught me the importance of every word I write and reminded me that: "It's the message, not the messenger, that is important." In this new work, I also want to thank Dr. Marshall Rosenberg, whose unending commitment to nonviolent communication is transforming our speech from one of judgment to one of compassion. Last, I want to thank all the many thousands of women and men who have taught me the realities of rape and dating communication. For all those survivors of rape, this book is for you and the courage you found to keep going and keep thriving. Your hope and faith in your ability to heal and be whole again has kept me going when I felt like giving up. God bless you all.

Contents

Introduction

S ince this book came out in 2000, I have seen the landscape change in regard to acquaintance rape. In the past years, there has been a date rape backlash that concentrated on debunking the figures quoted in this book (that were taken from the Ms. Study by Mary Koss). The essence of the backlash was that some people questioned the figures because some of the victims of date rape did not identify themselves as rape victims, even though legally they had sex against their will or without their consent. In pointing out that these women didn't call themselves rape victims, the proponents of the date rape backlash have claimed that these incidents were nothing more than morning-after regrets.

If you have ever been raped, you know that you desperately don't want to admit that it happened, especially if it's a date rape situation and if your rapist is popular. The humiliation and legal swamp that you have to tread to bring it to trial would make any woman stay in denial. If for argument's sake, however, we changed the situation to one of alcoholism, we realize that we have long accepted the fact that most alcoholics are in a constant state of denial about their drinking problem for years until they hit rock bottom. But denying you're an alcoholic doesn't make you sober, just as denying you've been raped doesn't make you any less of a rape victim. Certainly we have seen that most rapists deny that they committed rape. Does that make them innocent of the crime? No!

Violence is violence, regardless of who commits it or who believes it.

Rape is rape, whether the rapist or the rape victim is in denial. That's why we have a legal definition of rape, and that's why we have laws. We must continue to seek justice even when the criminal and the victim deny the crime because society demands that we do.

The reality is that to each and every woman, statistical figures don't really matter. Whether rape statistics indicate an increase or decrease in reported rapes, even one rape is too many, especially if it happens to you or to someone you love. We know that the vast majority of rape victims never report the crime. We hope they will, but even if they don't, we stand with them to protect them and to help them heal, even if they don't believe they were raped.

The question remains as to whether published figures for date rape are going up because these problems have become worse, or whether they're going up because more women are reporting them. There are many books, articles, and studies on the epidemic of sexual assault in the United States, most of which are statistical and address the issues after the fact—after the assault has taken place, after the violence has been committed. This book, though, is about prevention.

The challenge facing this book is how to reach women at all stages of life about the realities of sexual assault without scaring them into denial. The mere mention of the word rape causes many people so much discomfort that they want to either ignore the problem or to pretend it doesn't exist. It is for this reason that I have tried to simplify stories and other related crime prevention information from the most reliable and up-to-date sources into a concise guidebook for preventing sexual assault in all its forms, with the emphasis on date/acquaintance rape.

This book will explore a number of dangerous situations in which a woman might find herself being sexually assaulted. These situations include date/acquaintance rape, which is the main focus of this book, as well as stranger rape, sexual harassment, stalking, dating violence, and domestic violence. The book will touch on these areas, with the emphasis on prevention, and it will provide additional resources in the Resources section for those who wish a more in-depth discussion.

The information in this book is applicable to girls in high school, to women embarking on a college/university experience, and to mature women who are particularly vulnerable if they are reentering the dating process after being in a long-term relationship. Not all men are rapists, and not all women are rape victims. Unfortunately, however, acquaintance rape can happen to women of all ages and socioeconomic backgrounds, regardless of marital status or the length of time they've been in a relationship. (It is beyond the scope of this book to address rape within a marriage or rape in which the victim is male; however, the Suggested Reading section contains titles for reading material in those areas.)

Part of the difficulty in addressing the prevalence of date/acquaintance rape is that women tend not to be on their guard with men they know. There is a view of the rapist as a half-crazed maniac waiting in the bushes to pounce. Women in general take precautions against such an attacker, but statistics indicate that a woman is nearly five times as likely to be assaulted by someone she knows than by a stranger.

Contrary to the belief that rapists are hiding in the bushes or in the shadows of the parking garage, almost two-thirds of all rapes were committed by someone who is known to the victim. Sixty-seven percent of sexual assaults were perpetrated by nonstrangers; 47 percent of perpetrators were friends or acquaintances of the victims; 17 percent were intimate; and 3 percent were relatives (National Crime Victimization Survey, 2004[1]).

The issues of date and acquaintance rape first began to emerge on college and university campuses. Because of the prevalence of the problem for that age group, this book will focus frequently on prevention in the college or university setting. However, the tactics described are applicable to other settings and lifestyles as well.

Date/acquaintance rape prevention involves education, which must occur on two fronts simultaneously. Women need to learn the warning signs and how to extricate themselves from hazardous situations, and men must learn new attitudes towards women, including that "no" is "no," and that silence is not consent.

It will take time and effort on the part of parents and school personnel to change the way boys think about girls, and the way men think about women. Until that happens, girls and women will have to take a stronger stand for their rights to their own bodies. In truth, rape is a problem of male aggression, and only men can change their attitudes, but at the point where the confrontation occurs, it becomes the woman's problem. Women must act as if their parents, brothers, friends, and even the police will probably not be there to protect them. The nation's law enforcement agencies are not responsible for preventing crime and protecting the citizens of the United States. Their primary purpose is to enforce the law, apprehend criminals, and investigate crime after it happens. Regardless, there is much a woman can do to take responsibility for her own safety.

Reality Check:

Although many law enforcement agencies,
both federal and local, have fine crime prevention departments, it is up to you to do all that you can to prevent crime and keep yourself from becoming a victim.

This book is actually in many ways about choices. The choices a woman makes at the beginning of a date and subsequent relationship give her the options she will have as the situation progresses and the relationship matures. The more options she has, the more power she has, and the better her chances of getting out of a dangerous situation without being hurt.

It is important to understand that there is no one piece of advice that can be given to potential rape victims because each situation, each victim, and each perpetrator is different. If I were to tell a woman to physically resist with all her might by screaming, punching, and kicking, that advice would be ineffective if she tends to be passive and shy. She might not be able to bring herself to that action without getting hurt. If, however, she is very assertive and bold, it would be very difficult for her to be passive and nonconfrontational in a struggle, even if that might be the best thing to do. It's also true that screaming might be a very effective response in a populated location, but it would be a waste of time and energy in an isolated environment. There is no right or wrong thing to do in all criminal confrontations. It depends on many factors.

How, then, does a woman know what is right or wrong, what will work, and what will increase the attacker's violence? There are no guarantees. The best piece of advice I can give to girls and women is to take as many of the precautions outlined in this book as possible, and, in all circumstances, listen to your inner guidance and trust your instincts.

Sometimes, even with her best efforts, a woman is unable to stop her attacker. For that reason, this book includes information on the best way to proceed after it is too late for prevention. A woman who knows what to do next and what to expect from the process has a better chance of finding the help she needs to recover fully and in a shorter time.

Reality Check:
No matter what happens, rape is never the victim's fault.

This book is also about the choices a man makes in his relationships. Many men would never consider their own actions as rape, and yet they may press on even after a woman asks them to stop. Traditional attitudes hold a double standard that has some men seeing certain behaviors in women (such as how they dress or their willingness to drink or take drugs), as a sign that the woman is "asking for" sex. Men may also believe or assert that, once aroused, they are no longer in control of their sexual behavior. This is patently false. This book includes an Advice for Men chapter that explores such issues further.

Reality Check:
At any age or any stage of arousal, a man is in complete control of his sexual behavior.

I hope this book will not only educate, but will also motivate all women, whatever their ages, to be more aware, awake, alert, and committed with all of their might to not becoming victims.

This book will give you information about rape prevention, sexual harassment, stalking, dating violence, and nonviolent communication, but information without action will not make a difference in either a woman's or man's life. I sincerely hope you will choose to take action before your choices are limited or taken away. There is no time to waste.

Take action now by learning how certain behaviors can help keep you safe.

Take action now by reporting a rape if you have been the victim of one.

This book is not likely to change anybody's attitude overnight about the opposite sex or about his or her own gender. That can be done only through consistent education; but with the knowledge that this book has to offer, a young girl or woman might be able to recognize a dangerous man and/or situation before things get beyond her control.

This book also may be useful to men and boys and their fathers, who, consciously or unconsciously, have helped create an environment of rape and violence. In the final analysis, it is they who must stop the violence against women.

If even one rape is prevented as a result of this book, it will have served its purpose. However, it is my dream for the women of this nation that rape will disappear as an issue for them, and that men will understand that successful relationships are win/win, and that sex without consent is never an option. With that in mind, I have added a new chapter to this update. Chapter Seventeen: Nonviolent Communication, is an innovative guide to compassionate language that is transforming people all over the world. This is the next step in taking the violence out of our relationships. In its simple five-step process, it gives men and women real hope in transforming their language from one of attack/defense to one of compassion and understanding.

Date/Acquaintance Rape Prevention

Chapter One

Redefining Rape

R ape is a sexual assault in which a man uses his penis or other object
to commit vaginal, oral, or anal penetration—by force or by threat of
force—against another person's will, or when that person is physically
and/or mentally unable to give consent.

Date rape is simply a rape that happens between two individuals who
are dating.

Acquaintance rape is a rape that happens when the victim and perpetrator are already acquainted with each other. The majority of rapes are
actually acquaintance rapes, because in almost every case, the rapist gets to
know the victim at least enough for her to drop her guard. Once she lets
him into her confidence and begins to trust him, he strikes.

For the purpose of this book, I will include date rapes as acquaintance
rapes, since we can assume that people who date are acquainted. It is most
important to remember that even if you don't date, you are still a potential victim of rape.

It is important to realize that not every victim of rape will have signs of
physical abuse on her body. Just because her clothes are not shredded or
her bones aren't broken doesn't mean that she didn't resist or that she was-
n't raped. The threat of force is, in many cases, just as intimidating as
actual violence for the victim. The rapist uses fear to get control of her.

Even though rape is a life-threatening situation, the victim of acquaintance rape may not perceive it as such. The primary difference between

stranger rape and acquaintance rape is the relationship between the victim and the rapist. The fact that she supposedly knows the rapist at least superficially may make it more difficult for her to identify him as dangerous. This fact may also delude her friends and family into disbelieving her. Even more, knowing him can also dilute a woman's normal self-defense response to her attacker and cause her to hesitate in reporting the crime and seeking help for herself.

Acquaintance rape can happen to anyone who goes out on a date with or encounters a man who wants power over her in the form of sex and refuses to take no for an answer. Acquaintance rape accounts for 84 percent of all reported rapes[2], and yet it is estimated that only 5 percent of date/acquaintance rapes are reported.[3]

Is it possible that the most charming guy, who may be the leading quarterback for the high school football team, son of the mayor, president of the senior class, or the "perfect gentleman" who works or lives next door, may also be a rapist? Yes, he may commit the crime if he has the will to do it, the circumstances are right, and he thinks he can get away with it.

· ·

Reality Check:
After you say, "no," it is rape.

· ·

Many men's definition of rape does not apply to their own behavior or that of their male friends. Some men, as well as women, honestly believe that men cannot control themselves when they are sexually aroused. They believe the girl or the woman is responsible for both arousing and controlling the man. This is absolute rubbish. At any age, a man is perfectly able to control his sexual drive at any point, from first arousal to climax. But, the attitude that men are not responsible for their actions with women is not a new idea. Many men—young and old—still have the fantasy that once they are aroused they have a right to have sex with a woman, regardless of her wants, desires, or needs.

In a seminar at a prominent university fraternity, I was amazed at the attitude of the men I was addressing. When asked, "How many 'no's does it take before you finally stop your sexual pursuit?" the answer was, "Twenty or thirty." In fact, the president of the fraternity actually said, "If we give women the right to say 'no,' it gives them too much power." But this kind of attitude is not exclusive to young college males. I was shocked when I gave a similar talk at a local church's nondenominational singles' group. The participants were middle-aged, successful adults, including doctors, lawyers, and business executives. One actually stood up and said: "If a woman gets in my Mercedes without wearing a bra, she's asking for it!" Another man agreed, saying that any woman who goes up to a man's apartment, or allows a man into her apartment, is saying she wants to have sex. Such attitudes have been created and taught by fathers, grandfathers, and yes, even by mothers. Some women today still believe that it's a woman's job to control the man's behavior, and that women just have to tolerate the assaults.

Rape is about power. Men rape to get power over women. These men often feel powerless in their lives, and so they look for a way to increase their sense of self-worth by controlling and manipulating another "weaker" human being. Of course, this is a flawed idea, and rape doesn't give the rapist any lasting sense of power or self-worth, so he may continue to commit the crime until it becomes increasingly violent.

Let's be clear about this point of control. A woman is not responsible for keeping a man in control of his own sexual responses. Each man is responsible for his own actions, and, no matter what a woman does, he has no right to any sexual contact with her against her will or without her knowledge. Rape is not just "he said; she said." Rape is not just a misunderstanding or the result of a lack of communication. Rape is an act of choice to commit a crime and to forcibly obtain power over another individual through the means of sexual assault.

....

Reality Check:

Rape is not just a misunderstanding. Rape is a criminal act of choosing to overpower a woman and to have sexual intercourse with her without her consent or without her knowledge.

....

Chapter Two

What Makes a Woman Vulnerable

The term acquaintance rape is used today to mean any situation in which the assailant is merely known to the victim. It should be understood that just because a woman is not dating the perpetrator, that doesn't mean he can't be a rapist. Any man who has access to a woman can commit rape, including her doctor, lawyer, pastor, teacher, delivery man, salesman, brother, father, or friend.

Reality Check:
You are five times more likely to be raped by someone you know than by a stranger.

All women, regardless of their age, should remember that being desperate for companionship or willing to settle for any relationship in order not to be alone could lead to dangerous situations. Younger women put themselves at risk because they may not realize the potential for danger. Mature women may derive a false sense of security from their past dating experiences and may feel that they are now older and wiser.

Points of Vulnerability
A False Sense of Security

Acquaintance rape has touched nearly every college and university campus. Some educators, school officials, security staffs, and counselors are at a loss as to how to talk about stopping date rape without appearing to say that the university environment is unsafe. The reality is that a university is no more dangerous than any other high-density environment. However, many students approach this community environment with little or no awareness of the possible dangers.

First-year students are caught up with being on their own and away from home. Tragically, the thrill of that freedom supersedes the thought that crime, specifically sexual assault, can happen to them. Most of the time, the excitement of having her own place as well as the determination to "make it" without parental controls can silence the real dangers of being a single woman on her own. The euphoria of being independent—living away from home on a college campus—can create a false sense of security. For this reason, young women often get into situations, usually with alcohol and/or drugs, in which they become easy prey for more experienced men. It is common for students to take unnecessary risks while at school because they feel invulnerable and protected in the college environment. In addition, young women may also want to have a good time and party with alcohol just like the guys. This can be a dangerous mistake.

Some mature women believe that they can let their guard down because they have dated before. The dynamics of starting a new relationship can be very difficult, especially if the woman is dating again after a long time. Beyond the ready-made social environment of a university campus, it can be more difficult to meet eligible men to date. Loneliness or insecurity may drive a woman to go out with men she might not ordinarily consider a good match, or she might meet men through personal ads or at singles bars where she won't really know anything about them before the dating begins. To some degree, a mature woman can use this to her advantage, as she is less likely to think that she knows the man well after only a few encounters than a college student who may be fooled by the apparent safety of her campus environment. Although she may have had more dating experience, a more mature woman may have forgotten the realities of being with a stranger. Fears, insecurities, and family may complicate even the simplest of friendships. If she's going out with someone after a long marriage of say twenty or thirty years, she may find out quickly that times have changed. She will need to think about her own physical safety and take the same precautions that a younger woman should take.

A False Sense of Intimacy

To think that she knows a man after only one or two encounters, or after seeing him only in public, can place a woman in jeopardy. Familiarity breeds a dropping of one's guard. We all are taught as youngsters to fear strangers, but not to fear friends and acquaintances. Yet we are in far greater danger from those we know—or think we know—than we are from strangers. It is especially inconceivable to a young, naive woman that she could be assaulted by the very guy who shares her classes with her. Even a more mature woman—if she wants a relationship badly—will ignore her instincts and perhaps forgo her cautionary behaviors in order to give herself a green light for the relationship. Remember, you can never really know an individual well enough in one or two meetings. It is essential for a woman to observe a person in a variety of social situations over a period of time before allowing herself to be in a vulnerable situation with him.

Misleading Appearances

Appearances can be deceptive and are, unfortunately, not a foolproof indicator of what may be going on below the surface. According to statistical figures, the majority of rapists are middle-class white men. Neat clothing and grooming may be reassuring, but it is more important to inquire into a man's attitudes toward women and to carefully observe how he treats you.

The rapist desires power more than sex. We tend to think that men who are desirable and attractive can't be rapists, because if they are attractive they can get all the sex they want. Not true. It doesn't matter what he looks like, or even if he's married or in a relationship. This kind of man can be just as mixed up about sexual coercion as apparently less-desirable men are. The average rapist is not a twisted, ugly monster who lurks in the bushes. The average rapist looks like, and maybe is, the guy next door.

Drinking or Taking Drugs

The vast majority of acquaintance rapes involve abuse of alcohol and/or drugs. Chapter Six will give you more information on this subject. However, it is a fact that alcohol affects women differently from the way it affects men. This disparity is due mainly to three factors: body size, body composition, and levels of alcohol dehydrogenase enzyme. On average, women are smaller than men and carry more body fat, which contains little water to dilute alcohol in the bloodstream. In addition, women have less of the metabolizing enzyme alcohol dehydrogenase. Together, these differences between male and female physiology result in a higher concentration of alcohol in a woman's body than in a man's body for the same amount of alcohol ingested. A woman will, in most cases, become more intoxicated on less alcohol than a man.

Allowing Herself to Become Isolated

Criminals generally don't commit their crimes in view of the public. Likewise, a rapist will want to isolate his victim before he commits the crime. If a man attempts to commit sexual assault in a fairly public place, a woman stands a better chance of attracting attention and getting help than if she is alone with him. In order to prevent herself from becoming isolated, a woman must stay alert and plan ahead for how she would respond if the guy she is with shows signs of becoming dangerous. She must mentally prepare for that possibility.

Ignoring Warning Signals

What are the warning signals that a possible rapist sends when he intends to assault a woman? There is more to this than just the nagging feeling that she has in the pit of her stomach that something is wrong.

In his book *The Gift of Fear*, Gavin de Becker, one of the world's foremost violence prevention specialists, outlines the behaviors criminals use on women. He notes that you should be careful if the man you are with does any of the following:

- Behaves as if the two of you are more intimate than you really are, or uses a lot of "we" phrases and appears to be working too hard to make you trust him.

- Appears to be trying to charm you: He may try to disorient you or allure you. "Niceness is a decision, a strategy of social intercourse. It is not a character trait. It has been said that men are nice when they pursue; women are nice when they reject," says de Becker. Behaving in a way that is unusual or excessively ingratiating can be a sign that a man is attempting to manipulate or control you.
- Gives too many details about himself. If he is giving you information that you are not asking for, and that most people would not volunteer, he may be lying to you.
- Makes small criticisms, which offers you the opportunity to prove him wrong. For instance, if a man says: "You're so beautiful that you are probably stuck up and wouldn't go out with someone like me," he may be hoping you'll say to yourself: "I'm not a snob, and I'll prove him wrong by going out with him." This is manipulation, and the man may be trying to get you to think that going out with him is your idea, and that you have something to prove to him.
- Spends lavishly on you and appears to be expecting something in return. If the man is attempting to make you feel that you owe him something, you may be in for trouble.
- Makes unsolicited promises, such as, "I'll have just one drink, and then I'll go." An unsolicited promise can be a way to buy time or to give the man an opportunity to get control over you or the situation. If you have made it clear that you want your date to leave, and he says he'll leave "just as soon as I have another drink," or, "after I use the bathroom," or, "after I make a phone call," etc., you will have to be firm and communicate clearly and strongly your desire to leave or for him to leave.
- Attempts to control you. If your date is not allowing you to participate in decisions about the date, if he insists on ordering for you in a restaurant or "taking care of everything," or if he suggests that you don't trust him, these may be warning signals.
- Says derogatory things about women. Expressing an attitude that women are inferior to men, that women should obey men, or that women are responsible for a man's sexual response, can all be signs of trouble.

- Doesn't accept "no" for an answer. If he offers you a drink or suggests that you go somewhere with him, and continues to press you even after you say "no," you will have to be very firm and communicate very clearly. If he won't accept "no" for an answer on something small, he may not accept "no" in regard to sex, either.

Ignoring Her Inner Guidance

We live in a male-dominated culture that often debunks intuition and inner guidance. Women who trust their inner guidance may be ridiculed by men for not being logical and realistic. The truth is that your inner guidance or intuition is the most trustworthy and dependable barometer you have. The above manipulations and tactics that most criminals use also can be used by perfectly harmless men. So the problem is: how does a woman know when one or more of these techniques is being used by a man with dangerous intentions? The answer lies in her intuition. When it comes to danger, intuition is always right in at least two important ways: (1) It is responding to something real. (2) It has your best interests at heart.

The following levels of intuition will give you an idea of how intuition works. According to de Becker, your intuition builds from curiosity to hunches, to gut feelings, to doubt, to hesitation, to suspicion, to apprehension, and finally to fear. Fear is the most important and critical factor. If you feel fear in a situation, honor it.

The question then arises, "What makes a woman invulnerable?" It is not so much a question of invulnerability, because all of us are vulnerable to crime. It is rather a question of what makes a woman stronger and less likely to become a victim. The answer is knowledge, coupled with a determination to act in her own best interest, regardless of what others think or do. The following chapters will give you that knowledge. The determination to use it is up to you.

Chapter Three

One Woman's Story

Date rape generally does not happen out of the blue. In most cases there are warning signals and a progression of events that, if understood, shed some light on how the rapist operates and how the intended victim may have played right into his hands.

This story of one survivor is symptomatic of many of the things that can happen to a woman when her date/acquaintance refuses to honor her wishes and decides to take from her what she does not want to share. The story is divided into ten stages that serve to illustrate how this particular date rape progressed, from innocent first contact to assault, and finally to rape. Helen and Jim are aliases to protect the real names of the persons involved. Helen's story is only one example, but it contains many of the elements that frequently recur in incidents of date/acquaintance rape.

"I guess my story is not that unusual—many of my friends in college were also raped. We all suffered, and we continue to be traumatized by what happened to us during that time. I've since learned that rape victims like me take longer to heal because we've had our trust taken from us. It's difficult for me to trust men. I'm always thinking, What does he have on his mind? Will he rape me when my guard is down?"

Stage 1: Introduction and background. At this point, he may seem to be the perfect gentleman.

"Jim and I met during college. He was running for student body president, and I was one of the people in his campaign. He was enormously popular, and I guess I was as impressed as every other girl who was with him. I worked really hard to get him elected, and after the election he asked me out. We went to lunch."

Comment: In this first stage, Jim appears as the ideal man—successful, bright, an honor student, and tremendously popular.

Prevention: Helen thinks she knows him, but she actually knows only the public side of Jim. It is important to remember that even though you may have spent time with the person in class, at a party, at the office, or in a social situation, that doesn't mean you know all about him. He may be showing you only one side of his personality.

Jim and all men need to understand that what works in the business and sports arena doesn't always work in relationships. There is a tendency to believe that persistence and drive are the building blocks of success, that it is a win/lose world, in which the end justifies the means. Men need to realize that in relationships, a win/lose belief system is totally inappropriate and destructive.

Stage 2: His comments and attitudes about women surface. It may become obvious at this point that he does not really respect women.

"I didn't really hear some of the things that he said until I thought about them afterward. He made several remarks about women and how they tease men to get what they want and then complain when they get 'it.' I don't know why it didn't ring a bell in my head, but I guess I wasn't as much into the women's movement as I am today, so I let it pass."

Comment: Many women are in the habit of tolerating insensitive remarks made by men and ignoring their behavior. They often make excuses for men and will not confront such negative attitudes, even if the attitude is abusive. In this situation, Jim's comment seems to indicate that he sees women and men in an adversarial context—a kind of "them and us" perception.

Many men will reveal their true feelings and attitudes about women through their off-hand comments when their guard is down. They may say disparaging things about women and their bodies. Jim made an important statement about women teasing men with their bodies and then complaining when the man gets turned on. Jim made the common statement that many men with traditional attitudes make: A woman is responsible for the behavior of a man. This is a warning signal!

Jim also implied that a man will do what he wants, and that it is justified, especially if he feels that the woman has led him on to the point of no return. Jim is making the often-repeated statement that once a man gets turned on, he can't control himself.

....

Reality Check:
No one turns anyone else on. We turn ourselves on.

....

When Jim or any man gets visually turned on by another person, there is a tendency to believe that the other person did the turning on. This is not true. If you get sexually aroused by someone, then you did it to yourself with your thoughts. It is also true that if you can turn yourself on, you can turn yourself off as well. Jim is totally in control of his thoughts, feelings, and emotions. Helen has no part in the way his mind or body operates.

Prevention: Helen might have corrected him and stated that a man is responsible for his own behavior, regardless of a woman's actions. This would have communicated to Jim that she is not like some of the more passive women he may have dated. At this point, Jim might have made the decision that Helen would not be an easy target and might have changed his mind about the assault. Statements such as Jim's indicate that the man may feel disconnected from women. He may feel that he has to impose his personality and power over women. Such feelings are often expressed unconsciously in the course of a man's conversation, especially when he is relaxed and speaking in an unfiltered manner.

Stage 3: He treats you as if you are not his equal. He makes decisions for you and is obsessed with control.

"A couple of days later, we met for drinks in a restaurant/bar off campus. He immediately took charge of me and the whole evening. He insisted on ordering dinner for me. I was impressed with his sophistication and how the waiters catered to his commands. No wonder he was class president; he seemed born to command. Then, he started instructing me on exactly how to eat my dinner, saying he was tired of girls who didn't know proper etiquette. I was torn between feeling pampered by his attention and feeling totally unimportant at the same time, as if I had no opinion or knowledge about how to act. I now realize how all of this was only a means to control and intimidate me."

Comment: Remember that control is the issue here. Jim is testing the waters to see how Helen will respond. His "take charge" attitude may appear to be flattering to some women who want to be taken care of, but it is a danger signal that he wants to control you and your behavior. Often a man with traditional attitudes seems to need to control a woman and will go to almost any lengths to subdue her and/or convince his peers that the woman is under his control. He may equate his ability to subjugate women with feeling in control of his own life. In a marriage, this kind of man may insist on control of the bank account and finances as well as on making all of the major decisions. He may also deny his wife, whom he believes to be his property, the opportunity to work, to go to school, or even to have friends. He may be extremely jealous and publicly humiliate her in front of their friends. This kind of control often escalates into domestic violence.

Prevention: In retrospect, Helen saw Jim's behavior at this stage as controlling. If she had felt uncomfortable at the time, Helen could have insisted on ordering for herself. This might have communicated again to Jim that she's a woman with a mind of her own who cannot be controlled.

Remember, if you find yourself in this type of situation, you need to stay alert to your comfort level with his behavior. Keep in mind that accumulating controlling behaviors may be a warning signal. Continually gauge your own comfort level and inner guidance.

Stage 4: He plies you with alcohol and drugs—the assault begins! This is his attempt to reduce your ability to resist.

"We drank for a while, and I wasn't intending to drink too much, but he kept ordering for me and insisted that I drink up. At first I thought, 'Why not?' I didn't mind having a good time and, anyway, I trusted him. God, you know, he was student body president, and every girl in the place was kind of admiring me for who I was out with. I definitely remember thinking, 'Why is he doing this? Why does he want me to drink so much?'

I wasn't really sure what was going on during all this, but back then everyone in our class got drunk at least once a week anyhow, so it was probably no big deal. I don't know what happened to me after that. I think I blacked out. I was really drunk."

Comment: Alcohol is a great enabler of violent behavior. It tends to break down the inhibitions in both men and women. In many cases, getting drunk is a prelude to being unable to stop an assault that may come later. In some cases, the perpetrator will not drink as much as his intended victim. This is because he knows that too much alcohol inhibits sexual performance.

Jim was very obvious in his desire for Helen not only to drink, but to become intoxicated. Many men still think that the reason a woman drinks is to "loosen up." He feels he needs an advantage, and alcohol is his advantage. Helen made the statement that everyone in her class got drunk at least once a week. The most common reason for drinking in college is not to loosen up, but to get drunk.

Prevention: Drinking and drugs play an important part in the commission of rape because if you drink or take drugs, you run the risk of numbing your senses and making yourself confused. Alcohol reduced Helen's chances to prevent the crime. The more she drank, the less control she had—over her mind and body. Often, by the time a woman realizes what has happened, it's too late to take significant preventive action. Stay alert and aware of what's happening around you and in your own mind. It is very important to recognize your alcohol limit as well as the consequences you may face when you go beyond that limit. Helen could have refused to go beyond her own limit. She could have ordered for herself, insisting that she not drink to excess or just not drink at all.

··

Reality Check:
Alcohol has been shown to be a significant factor in the vast majority of acquaintance rapes, and in more than 90 percent of all campus crime.

··

What a man needs to understand is that if he is successful in getting the woman drunk, he puts himself in jeopardy with the law, because if the woman is incapable of saying no, getting away, or even resisting his advances, then he is, by law, committing a crime.

If you don't drink liquor or take drugs at all, you are less likely to be incapacitated and confused during an acquaintance rape situation.

Stage 5: He manipulates you into an isolated area. Now you are alone. The security you may be depending upon (a party or gathering of friends) no longer is there.

"The next thing I remember, I was in his truck, and he was taking me to his place. He kept saying not to worry because there would be a lot of people there, a party of some kind, and anyway he said he'd take care of me. I didn't know at the time what he really meant. But I would soon find out. I wasn't feeling too hot at the time. Drinking too much gives me a headache. I told him that I might throw up. He said I'd better not; it was a brand new truck. It didn't matter to him, he just kept driving. When we got there, I didn't see any other cars, and that's the first time that voice inside me said, 'Get out,' but I was so drunk that I couldn't think straight. God, I should have listened to that voice. He said that maybe the people had parked somewhere else, and they were probably waiting for us. Somehow I knew he was lying."

Comment: Criminals depend upon isolation to commit their crimes. Yes, this is a crime about to happen, and he is a criminal when he commits that crime. It is imperative that you not become isolated or be alone with him unless you absolutely trust him. Jim did what many men would do when they are planning to rape. They must have unlimited access to their intended victim without interference. Criminals use various means to trick their unsuspecting victims into positions of vulnerability. Helen thought she would be safe because she was supposedly going to a party with lots of other people. She was tricked.

Prevention: At this stage, a woman needs to be alert for inconsistencies that could lead to isolation. If there was a party that Jim wanted to attend, why didn't he mention it earlier at the start of the evening? Helen could have questioned him about the party.

Once you're in his car, your options are limited. It's always a good idea to take your own car and meet him wherever you are going. That way you have control over your escape. Had she not been drinking, Helen could have insisted on taking her own vehicle.

In most traumatic situations, especially crimes, potential victims recall having sensed some kind of warning signal. (The warning signal may be an inner voice, a vision, or just a feeling of dread or impending doom.) How important is that voice or feeling? It is absolutely imperative that you listen to it and take action, heeding the warning that your intuition is giving you. As soon as Helen sensed that Jim was lying to her, she could have insisted on going home.

Stage 6: Confusion and limited escape.

"Why did I go in? When we got upstairs, of course there was no one there, I knew it! He was all over me from the moment we got inside the door. He said, 'You've been teasing me all evening.' He started ripping my clothes, saying, 'I gotta have it; I gotta have it,' like 'it' was something not connected to me, a thing that wasn't human. I tried to talk to him. I said, 'No, not this way; I don't want to.' He wasn't listening to me! I just couldn't believe this was happening to me. He was so popular. He was an honor student. He was student body president. I said, 'This can't happen to me. Stop it, please! Let me go! I want to go home.' I told him if he didn't let me go, I would be sick. He laughed and slapped me. He said that if I made a mess, I'd have to clean it up. ·

"When he slapped me, I knew I was in big trouble. I tried to get away from him, but I didn't know where I was. I realized I had left my purse in his truck, and I certainly couldn't ask him for a ride home now. I kept thinking about how I was trapped there with him with no way home."

Comment: Confusion has led to denial that the situation is happening to her. In many cases of acquaintance rape, precious seconds and minutes are lost while the intended victim is going through denial. Over and over, she may question herself and the choices she made that evening that have brought her to that point. This process comes from our unending need to understand what is happening to us. We keep asking ourselves, "Why is this happening? What did I do wrong? Why did I go out with him? Why didn't I listen to my guidance?" and finally, "Why is he doing this?"

You do not have the luxury at this moment to try to figure out why all this is happening. There are no simple answers anyway. Now is the time to act and act quickly.

. . . .

Reality Check:

It is important to understand that no matter what choices you make in a dating situation, you did not choose to be raped.

. . . .

The rapist has taken that choice away from you. He is the one who has chosen to commit a violent crime.

The alcohol added to Helen's confusion at this point as well as her inability to believe what was happening to her. She had trusted Jim. He was the opposite of a stereotypical rapist in every sense of the word. All the reasons why he couldn't be the kind of person to rape flashed through her mind—honor student, student body president, and, of course, a very popular person. After all, if the other students liked him so much then he couldn't be doing this, right? Wrong! This confusion is also common with assaults committed by older, more established men. If a man is successful in business, can he be a rapist? Yes. If a man is rich and has prestige, can he be a rapist? Yes. If a man is in a position of trust and moral authority (such as a doctor, lawyer, or minister), can he be a rapist? Yes.

Helen was in a state of denial at this point, and that state didn't change until Jim slapped her. Once he had slapped her, the reality of her situation came crashing in on her. Even though she tried to get away, it was too late. Her options were limited. As in most crimes, the best time to escape is within the first few moments of a confrontation. The longer you wait, the less control you are likely to have. It is within these first few seconds or minutes that the criminal probably is not yet in total control, so your options for escape could succeed if you can stop thinking and start acting.

Prevention: There aren't many options open to Helen at this point. The question is how can a woman cope with the mounting confusion she might experience in a situation like this, and, most importantly, how can she prevent the confusion from overtaking her.

First of all, breathe! Fear tends to stop your breathing, and that causes less oxygen to reach your brain, which contributes to the confusion. Confusion also stems from being unable to make decisions. You must, at this very critical moment, empty your mind of all the "what-ifs." Your only task is to escape. You don't have time to mull over all of the choices you made or the "Why is this happening to me?" questions. Tell your mind to stop thinking about that, and concentrate on survival.

The most common reason people fail to use weapons or martial arts training for self-defense is that they keep analyzing the risks versus the benefits. By the time they are through mulling things over, they have lost control of the situation. You must simplify your thinking and your actions in a situation like this; shut down your analytical thoughts. Your life is on the line; you must act decisively with 100 percent commitment to your own well-being.

Stage 7: He threatens you with physical violence or verbally abuses you to get you to cooperate.

"I just didn't know what to do. I screamed at him that he had no right to do this. He said: 'You're all alike, all of you! You lead a man on, and then this happens. You complain and scream bloody murder that it's not what you want. It's what you wanted all along! I saw you looking at me when I was giving all those speeches. You're just playing hard to get. Well, go ahead and play hard to get, 'cause now it's hard, and you're gonna get it!'"

Comment: Jim's words begin to express hatred and pent-up frustration at women. There are a number of cases where a man has committed rape when a "triggering event" happened. This triggering event may be an incident that reminds the man of past troubles with a woman. In that kind of rape, the current rape victim represents someone else, or all women in general. Jim may have been taking out years of misunderstandings and hurt feelings on Helen. He may even have been, in his mind, raping someone else. The point is, there is no way for a woman to know whether she is triggering this kind of response. It has nothing to do with her, therefore she can in no way be considered responsible for the man's behavior.

Most reported acquaintance rapes are committed with minimal to moderate acts of violence. The rapist generally depends on his physical size and weight to control his victim, without resorting to the additional brutality that in the majority of cases accompanies stranger-to-stranger rape.

Jim had actually already used mild violence on Helen, and he had made it clear that he would do whatever was necessary to get what he wanted. He justified what he did and what he intended to do. For many women, the threat of violence is so shocking, especially coming from a guy they trusted, that they freeze and find it almost impossible to take action to defend themselves. Whether the man uses physical violence, emotional force, or intimidation on a woman, it still steals her ability to choose.

Reality Check:

The threat of violence is just as intimidating and paralyzing as violence itself! A woman being raped, overwhelmingly and accurately, believes that her life is in danger. For this reason, Dr. Peg Ziegler, former director of the Atlanta, Georgia, Rape Crisis Center, has called the crime of rape the "unfinished murder."

Prevention: At this point Helen might have been able to turn the tables on Jim if she had pulled out all the stops and physically fought him rather than submit. Fighting back against an acquaintance rapist is a viable alternative; unfortunately , many women don't believe a rape is happening until it's over.

Stage 8: The actual assault or rape. After the assault, he may minimize his actions or question the importance you have placed on the assault, i.e., he acts as if nothing had happened.

"After he raped me, he acted as if it was my fault. He said, 'You know, you really shouldn't turn a guy on like that. You could get hurt.' I couldn't believe what he was saying. It was as if he had become a father-figure, all protective and concerned about my welfare. He kept talking to me, trying to make conversation. It was as if nothing had happened. He actually helped me get dressed. I was so torn up inside that I was shaking. I couldn't keep from crying. He drove me home, and all the way he was talking and advising me to be careful and not to trust strangers around here because it wasn't safe. I didn't say anything. I was still in shock. I went up to my room and just sat there holding myself. I remember rocking back and forth, like when I was little. He called me later that night and said that maybe we should go out next week. He actually thanked me for a wonderful night and said he'd see me tomorrow in biology class."

Comment: Jim did what many acquaintance rapists do after the assault: he behaved in a conciliatory manner toward his victim. He helped Helen get dressed, acted concerned about her safety, and drove her home. He called her later that night to thank her. This might seem like two separate men. But it serves only to point out the dichotomy of beliefs that some men have about women and about their own sexual behavior. It is apparent that Jim did not understand that he had committed rape.

Jim's behavior is consistent with what the FBI calls "The Gentleman Rapist" or "Power Reassurance Rapist." Though he is certainly no gentleman, the FBI uses the term because this rapist tends to use low levels of force and to rely on threats of violence. He fantasizes that he and the woman are just having sex, and that is why he may later thank her for a "wonderful night." He pursues the relationship, apparently not comprehending that he has committed a crime. If the woman charges him with rape, he will be totally confused and in a high state of denial.

Prevention: It is important to understand that the ultimate source of rape prevention is with the man. Jim's determination to get control, his need to feel power, his lack of understanding and compassion for Helen, and his disregard for the law and what is right are the issues that need to be addressed. Attempts at analysis and understanding of Jim's behavior are, in reality, a waste of time, especially for Helen. For her, it doesn't matter what or who drove him to commit rape.

· ·

Reality Check:
At some level the rapist made a choice to commit a violent crime and probably thought he could get away with it.

· ·

Helen could have emphatically told Jim that she would report him to campus security if he didn't stop what he was doing. However, she might not have wanted to aggravate him before or after the rape by telling him she planned to report it. If the full impact of what he was about to do had been pointed out to him, he might have stopped himself, but there is also a chance that a rapist may resort to physical violence to ensure a woman's silence. Although after the assault it is too late for prevention, reporting the incident can possibly contribute to stopping future rapes by this man.

Stage 9: After the assault, the symptoms may continue for many years. The most important bond—trust—has been broken. Self-criticism, guilt, and self-hatred may follow as the victim tries to understand what happened, and why.

"I didn't go to biology class the next day. I left school and went home to my parents, but I couldn't tell them. I knew they wouldn't understand. My parents are good Catholics; they hardly even drink. I just couldn't take their guilt. I had enough of my own. I left school. I just couldn't go back. He was so popular, so respected by everybody that I just thought no one would ever believe me. You know today, ten years later, I still haven't told my parents. Maybe if it happened today, I wouldn't leave school because there's more awareness about date rape. Now it seems like everyone's talking about it. I'm glad. Several years later, I talked with some of the girls with whom I went to school and they told me he had raped several girls, and no one ever reported it. I think the guy's an attorney today."

Comment: One of the most common consequences of an acquaintance rape is that the perpetrator continues his life unaffected—at least on the surface—while the survivor is barely able to put the pieces of her life back together. Her life is ruined, and his is unmarked. It is for this reason that women should think very carefully about reporting the crime. In many cases, a woman will be able to recover faster if she has acknowledged the incident, filed a police report, and pressed charges. If she can do this, difficult as it is, she may feel less guilty about the situation and honestly feel that there's only one criminal person at fault, and it's not her. Of course, in order to facilitate the healing process, she must get help and support from therapists and other support groups. This will let her know that she is not alone and that there are people who care. It must also be said that had the other women that Jim had raped reported it, Helen may never have been assaulted.

For Helen, as for so many women, the trauma lasted for years. She quit school and, even to this day, she is affected in her relationships with men, though it has been many years since the rape took place. Some psychologists have said that the trauma and broken trust after an acquaintance rape linger for many years.

A woman raped by a stranger may not have to deal with the trust issue to the same degree. A woman raped by someone she knows and trusts is in a doubly difficult situation. She also may not be believed by friends, relatives, and authorities. Not being believed may add to her feelings of betrayal, worthlessness, guilt, and loneliness. It may cause her to bury her feelings altogether and pretend that the crime never happened, which can cause severe long-term damage, both emotionally and physically.

· ·

Reality Check:
You can recover and heal after a rape,
but only if you survive the assault.

· ·

Hindsight is always 20/20, and it is vital for the survivor of rape to understand that there are no right or wrong choices. If you are attacked and survive, then you did the right thing, no matter what you did. Your top priority in the attack is to survive. Stop the rape if you can; if you can't, then your next goal is to survive and to heal.

There is help for women who have been raped. Support groups have sprung up all over the country to help women deal with this trauma and recover their feelings of self-worth. There are thousands of sites available on the internet for you to get connected with people and organizations who care. If you don't have a computer, go to a friend who has internet access or use the computer at your local library. There are many caring and qualified therapists and support groups that can help in the healing process.

Don't try to deal with it alone. Get help from people who will believe you and not judge you. You are not alone!

Chapter Four

The Date Rape Triangle

Regardless of where it takes place, the crime of date rape involves three factors, which I call "The Date Rape Triangle."

Criminal Intent—more than half of all rapes are clearly planned.

Alcohol/Drugs—on many occasions, the woman becomes physically immobilized to the degree that she has consumed alcohol and/or drugs.

Isolation—the criminal generally must get his victim to a place where there are no witnesses.

Diagram 1: The Date Rape Triangle

Once these three factors come together, escape is limited and an acquaintance rape may happen.

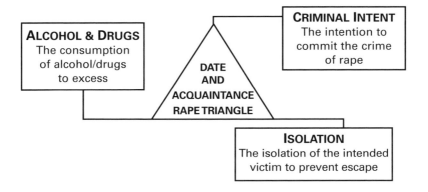

ALCOHOL & DRUGS
The consumption of alcohol/drugs to excess

CRIMINAL INTENT
The intention to commit the crime of rape

DATE AND ACQUAINTANCE RAPE TRIANGLE

ISOLATION
The isolation of the intended victim to prevent escape

···

Reality Check:
Rape can happen to anyone, regardless of her behavior and circumstances.

···

In most cases, however, the potential victim of acquaintance rape has the ability to control two out of three of the acquaintance rape triangle factors. She can control how much alcohol and/or drugs she consumes, and whether she becomes isolated and alone with the rapist. If she can break just one side of the acquaintance rape triangle, she will greatly reduce her chances of becoming a victim, but remember there are no guarantees.

Planning Ahead

Crime victims who fare the worst in a confrontation with a criminal generally have one thing in common. Each thought it would never happen to them, took no precautions, or even gave any thought to protecting themselves.

It may help you in the long run to put yourself hypothetically in the position of being attacked, asking yourself, "If he did this, what would I do?" It's a way of rehearsing the situation before it ever occurs, so you can make some plans or preparations. You might give some thought to this for a few minutes while you prepare for a date. It seems unappealing, but it can make all the difference if the worst should come to pass.

Questions to Ask Yourself

What if you see signs that a location or party is high risk for women? What would you do?

What if he is not all he said he was? What would you do?

What if he tried to rape you? What would you do?

What if you could not get home? What would you do?

What if you could not fight back because you were drunk? What would you do? Could you get away?

If you did get away, where would you go?

How would you get help?

Who could you call in an emergency?

Take the time and write down some answers to these hypothetical questions, and what you might do to change the outcome. The more you have considered what might happen in various situations and how you would respond, the better prepared you are.

Fifteen Ways to Prevent Acquaintance Rape

1. Communicate up front with him. If you want a platonic relationship, say so. If there is to be no sex, say so.
2. Be assertive with him about sex; he can't read your mind.
3. Make sure that your body language matches your words.
4. Wear clothes and shoes that allow full range of movement and in which you can move quickly if you must.
5. Introduce him to your roommate, friends, or family before you go out, and tell them when you will return.
6. If this is the first time you and he are getting together, meet him during daylight hours and take your own car with you.
7. Remember that isolated spots can be dangerous. Meet him in public and stay around other people.
8. Fraternity rush parties and all parties where there is excessive alcohol consumption can be dangerous. Do not go to isolated bedrooms or basements, and do not allow yourself to be alone with men with no other female present.
9. Alcohol and drugs are tools that rapists use to subdue their victims. Getting high or drunk will make his job easier and your escape more difficult.
10. Always pour your own drinks, even if you are drinking only soft drinks. Never let someone else carry or watch your drink for you. If you have any reason to suspect that your drink has been spiked, throw it away and remove yourself from the situation.

11. Always carry a telephone calling card, or better yet a cellular phone, and enough cash to get help and get home. If you need to make a call for help and it is at all possible, excuse yourself and go to the women's bathroom or some other safe place to make your call. Do not do it where he can hear your conversation.
12. Never leave a bar or party with a man you do not know or are not absolutely sure about.
13. Take a self-defense course in order to raise your self-confidence and learn many precautions that you can take that are suited to your individual personality. (Note that in order to actually be able to successfully defeat an attacker in a confrontation, you will probably need more than one lesson.)
14. Be aware of what is happening around you, and trust your instincts. Do not let a man intimidate you or make you feel uncomfortable. If your inner guidance tells you to leave, do so at once.
15. Have a plan in your mind that you can follow if your date gets abusive or dangerous. Remember that your best chance to escape is at the beginning of the confrontation. Don't delay or second-guess yourself. Commit to your own safety and do whatever you have to do to escape. Don't worry about what other people may think about you if you feel you are in danger. Act and act quickly.

Chapter Five

Danger Spots

Helen's story illustrates many of the most common elements of date rape, but remember that date and acquaintance rape can happen anywhere and anytime of day or night. In most cases of rape, the intended victim let down her guard for a moment or longer, which gave the rapist enough time to get control of the situation and prevent her escape. This can happen in a parking lot, a hallway, on the street, in a car, or in a home. There are three danger spots that women should be particularly aware of: bars, fraternity houses, and college athletic parties.

Bars

Meeting men in bars is obviously hazardous for any woman. Many men go to bars primarily to meet women, and the women that they meet there, are, in their opinion, available. Alcohol and bars attract what some men call "bad" girls and "loose" women. The mere fact that you are there presupposes, in their minds, that you are available for or asking for sex. In addition, in the majority of date/acquaintance rapes, alcohol and drugs play a part in breaking down the resistance of the woman, as well as releasing the male's inhibitions. Be extra cautious with any man you meet in a bar.

Fraternity Houses

Fraternity houses can be a particular danger spot for college-aged women.

A fraternity house can be a breeding ground of hyped-up masculinity and machismo. There is a strong sense of bonding and competition among the guys that may result in unexpectedly aggressive behavior. A first-year female student is usually more vulnerable because she does not know the facts about campus life, and she may also not be familiar with the hot spots on campus or the reputations of some men who, if given the chance, will take advantage of her. She is also vulnerable because she has just left home, wants to make a good impression with the most popular guys on campus, and may drink to excess just to go along and be accepted.

· ·

Reality Check:

The most dangerous time for a woman in her first year of college occurs from move-in day to the first holiday break. This is when most rush parties happen.

· ·

Rush Week is a time of much excitement on campus. The fraternities are busily involved in getting new members, and there are usually a great number of parties. Unfortunately, where there are parties there may be alcohol and drugs. Some fraternities have what they call "Little Sisters," although some Greek fraternities and college administrations have now outlawed them and most fraternities have discontinued this practice. Little Sisters are generally first-year female students who help the fraternities during Rush Week. These Little Sisters often become "little victims" because they end up as the prime targets for acquaintance and gang rape.

A study in *Gender* magazine distinguished two types of fraternity houses: high-risk and low-risk. Among the women surveyed, most identified some fraternities as having more sexually aggressive members, where there is a higher probability for becoming a rape victim. These same women, however, considered other fraternity houses as "safe" or low-risk houses, where a woman could go to party and feel secure that she would not be in danger.

High-Risk Fraternity Houses

Without going into a great deal of psychological analysis of why some fraternity houses are more dangerous than others, here are some things to watch out for:

Uneven gender ratios at parties: Some parties have more men than women; others have more women than men.

Gender segregation: Men and women in different groups. Many men drinking together at a bar area.

Men treat women disrespectfully: They will often engage in jokes, conversations, and behaviors that degrade women, i.e., rating women's bodies from one to ten, or with thumbs up or thumbs down.

Bathrooms are filthy: The toilets often will be clogged, with vomit in the sink.

The atmosphere is less friendly: Men and women rarely smile or laugh. Men are openly hostile and threatening. There may be profanity, touching, pushing, or name-calling by men and women.

Gender self-consciousness: Students at high-risk parties seem self-conscious about women being there, and there is awareness that the atmosphere is sexually charged.

Dancing changes around midnight: Dancing early in the evening is often just between women, and around midnight couples start dancing erotically.

Propositions for isolation begin: The men will try to pick up the women and use some excuse to get them isolated.

Breakfast bragging: The day after a party at a high-risk house will often start with the brothers bragging about how many women they had sex with.

Low-Risk Fraternity Houses

Although these houses are, according to the survey, less risky, that should not give women a false sense of safety and license to drop their guard. You still need to watch the alcohol consumption, guard your drink so that it cannot be tampered with, and be careful of isolation. In general, low-risk fraternities are more likely to exhibit the following characteristics:

1. *Equal number of women and men at parties.*
2. *Social atmosphere is friendly with interaction between women and men.*
3. *Men and women dance in groups and together.*
4. *Many couples are in relationships and display affection.*
5. *Friendly conversation within coed groups.*
6. *Appearances that many people know each other.*
7. *When pushing occurs, participants tend to apologize.*
8. *Bathrooms are usable and well-supplied.*

It is apparent that the differences between high-risk fraternity houses and low-risk houses can give you signals about the kind of behavior that is likely to occur during a party. If you find yourself at a high-risk fraternity party, it might be wise to find a way to leave as soon as possible before something happens.

Progress at Fraternities

The alcohol-soaked fraternity culture is beginning to change. As legal liability and bad publicity soar in the wake of high-profile rapes and alcohol-related hazing deaths, fraternities are taking action. Some national fraternities say local chapters will be required to go "dry" within a few years. Across the nation, colleges have established "relationship agreements" with their fraternities specifying higher expectations and responsibilities. According to the National Interfraternity Conference in Indianapolis, Indiana, which represents sixty-six men's fraternities nationwide, "there is a genuine desire among fraternity leaders to change the culture, particularly in chapters focused on hedonism and alcohol."

In keeping with this, the University of Delaware's faculty senate's disgust over hazing and drinking violations nearly drove them to ban Greek Rush. Instead, the school created the Five-Star Program, which grades fraternities and sororities annually in five audited areas: academics, financial management, university and community service, campus involvement, and new-member education. Where once fraternities had open kegs at rush parties, "Dry Rush" is now the norm at many universities.

College Sports Celebrations

Whereas fraternities have had to make changes in their behaviors or face the possibility that the university would close chapters or ban them altogether, athletic groups and events, which can be even more dangerous, have in most cases avoided change. The reason lies in the prestige that a winning football or basketball team brings to the university and the alumnae dollars that go along with a championship season.

Male athletes can be particularly dangerous if given the right situation and sufficient alcohol to loosen inhibitions. Some athletes view relationships like opponents on the field, as adversaries. They have a high status on campus and are trained and rewarded for aggression. The male bonding that is natural in team sports can contribute to gang rape. Athletes may be protected by their coaches and the university, and kept from facing the consequences of actions such as drunkenness or assault if they are valuable to the team.

Danger Spot Prevention

Many of the precautions that apply to date rape also apply to social situations that may end up being danger spots.

Consider that the same warning signs in terms of male behavior exist in high-risk bars, fraternity parties, and sports or athletic celebrations. Be cautious and do not allow yourself to become isolated with one man or with a group of men. Generally, women, especially younger ones, tend to think that they're safer if they are in a group. This is true only if there are other females in the group.

Since alcohol and drugs are rape enablers, you should be very cautious about your consumption, especially if you notice any of the high-risk signs.

Remember that a drug can be slipped into your drink when you are not looking. Do not let your drink out of your sight or control, and do not drink it if you have any doubts whatsoever.

Keep your wits about you. Be aware of what is happening, and be prepared to escape and get to safety if your inner voice tells you to do so.

Chapter Six

Alcohol and Drugs: The Rape Enablers

Many people still believe that alcohol and drugs can make for great times both on and off campus. However, there are inherent dangers that come not only from accidents and overdoses, but also from changes in behavior that contribute to rape.

It is important to understand what happens to people when they drink and take drugs. It is also important to see and understand the relationship of alcohol and drugs to date rape.

Reality Check:
Alcohol is not an aphrodisiac. Alcohol is a depressant.
Too much alcohol inhibits male sexual performance
and a woman's ability to fight back.

About 75 percent of the men and more than half of the women involved in date/acquaintance rapes had been drinking or taking drugs before the attack.[6] In addition, alcohol is a contributing factor in the vast majority of campus crimes. Thus it is doubly important for universities to take action to curb excessive alcohol consumption on campus and at school-sponsored activities. According to a nationwide scientific study, approximately 86 percent of all college students drink,[7] and the main reason given for drinking by college students was to get drunk.[8]

From what I have learned from those who attend my seminars, many men are sexually inhibited, and alcohol has gained a reputation as a sexual stimulant simply by contributing to the loss of inhibitors. However, large amounts of alcohol can have disastrous effects on sexual performance. This is why a man who is planning a rape later in the evening will ply his companion with lots of alcohol, constantly refilling her glass, but will not drink so much that he himself becomes drunk.

The Effects of Alcohol

In addition to its physiological effects, alcohol also has a tendency to release inhibitions and make it easier to break customs or inner codes of behavior, leading to actions people would never take while sober. In other words, alcohol may tend to shut down the conscience in some people and give courage to others. Psychological research indicates that we all have a wall or barrier—a code of ethics and morality—that we won't cross. Alcohol seems to confuse the line, and it may drive an individual to do things he or she would normally never do. Alcohol can and does affect some men's perception of women. That influence can lead to violence in some individuals.

Alcohol complicates the situation for a number of reasons. Firstly, men who hold traditional, double standard attitudes may believe that a woman who is willing to drink or take drugs with them can't be a "good girl"and must be the kind of person who also will go along with sex. A woman's willingness to drink or take drugs in and of itself may cause the man to believe that the woman is "asking for it." He may believe that this places the responsibility for the rape on the woman and not on himself. (This double standard never faults men who drink, take drugs, and sleep around.)

Secondly, alcohol or drug consumption causes a woman's senses to become dulled and clouded. In a sexual assault, she is going to need all of her wits about her to be able to get out of the situation. Many times, a woman is too intoxicated to understand where the rapist is taking her or even what he's going to do until it's too late, and the assault has begun. Once the assault has reached the advanced stages, her options are severely limited, and her chances of stopping him could be all but gone.

I urge you to look at alcohol differently. This is not just a harmless recreational beverage, but a potent drug that can become a tool for rapists.

....

Reality Check:
You don't have to drink, take drugs, or be sexually active to have friends or to have a happy social life.

....

If your personal morals or code of behavior would keep you celibate and sober, don't let anyone pressure you to betray your own principles. Women who don't drink and don't sleep around obviously are less likely to be caught in a potential rape situation, but never believe that it can't happen to you.

Dulled Senses
When you go out with a guy, you will have to depend on your feelings. Pay attention to the inexplicable instincts that tell you at times
"Watch out!"
"There's something wrong with him!"
"He's not treating me with respect!"
"I don't feel comfortable with him anymore!"
"I'm starting to feel afraid. I want to go home!"
"I think I've made a terrible mistake!"

In many cases of sexual assault, the victim had a feeling that something was going to happen or that the perpetrator was going to hurt her. There may be times when his behavior is not obvious enough for her to put her finger on why he makes her uncomfortable—she may have a nagging feeling that something is wrong with him. She may have thought that she was being silly and brushed off her feelings with "Oh, this is nonsense." He comes from a good family. He's an upper-classman. He's an honor student. He's so good-looking. He's so popular. I should feel honored to be out with him. Alcohol consumption may confuse the validity of the inner voice, while making it difficult to take appropriate defensive maneuvers. She may have ignored her instincts and gone ahead with his plans for the evening. This decision can be a dangerous mistake.

Garbled Communication

All successful relationships are based on communication. In a dating situation, the woman may not have had much time to get to know the man yet. It can be dangerous to be coy, vague, or subtle. A woman must be absolutely clear and precise in what she wants from the date and what she expects from the relationship. This may seem like cold and manipulative behavior, but the consequences of poor understanding and bad communication can be devastating.

The woman's words, body language, and gestures are all that she has to get the point across to the man. Alcohol tends to garble people's words, and heavy drinking affects the hearing to a great extent. You may have noticed that when people get drunk, they tend to raise their voices. This is not only because some of their inhibitions are gone, but because the alcohol causes their hearing to become less acute.

Confusion and Disorientation

Alcohol affects the brain. It alters reality and changes the way you perceive what's going on around you. It not only makes the situation less uncomfortable, but it can also produce confusion and disorientation.

Confusion can become a major barrier to getting out of a dangerous acquaintance rape situation. You already are confused because you thought you knew this guy. You do not understand why he is doing this to you. You may not believe or refuse to believe what is happening to you because it is so unexpected. This sense of denial that you feel can seriously delay your defensive actions—if you can't accept what is happening to you, then you won't do anything to stop it or try to escape.

Rape can happen to anyone, and, yes, it can happen to you!

You may be saying to yourself, "Rape happens only in cities, to other people, with strangers who jump out of bushes. Rape doesn't happen to college students who come from good families; who are respectable and who don't sleep around. Rapists are not good-looking guys with 4.0 grade-point averages. Rapists are not upperclassmen. Rapists are not fraternity brothers who are supposed to take care of you. Rape can't happen to me, can it?" Yes! Yes! Yes! It can happen.

You may be saying rape happens only to young girls, to young women who are attractive and desirable. Rapists are not middle-aged men, successful businessmen, lawyers, doctors, ministers. Rape can't happen to me; I'm middle-aged. I'm divorced. I'm widowed. I'm not beautiful. It can't happen, can it? Yes! Yes! Yes! It can happen.

All of these preconceived notions are major causes of confusion during an acquaintance rape situation. Adding alcohol raises the victim's confusion even more. Alcohol may also add to feelings of disorientation that she may already be experiencing as a new college student getting used to a new environment, new roommate/s, and new rules and restrictions.

Often when an acquaintance rape occurs, the victim is brought to a strange place. She may feel trapped and lost, not knowing how to get home or even how to get out of there. She may feel dependent for guidance and/or transportation on the man or men accompanying her, even if they are actually going to rape her. This feeling of being trapped is difficult enough to deal with without adding alcohol.

Impeded Self-Defense

Alcohol saps your strength and makes you weaker than you normally are. It takes a tremendous amount of strength to fend off a physical or sexual attack by a man or men. He is probably bigger, taller, and stronger than you, and, although most date rape situations do not involve the use of a lethal weapon by the rapist, the size, weight, and strength of his body is weapon enough. You may have to kick him, slap him, run from him, or do any combination of things that could possibly deter him. You will need all your strength.

He will probably not be drinking as much as you because he knows he will need his strength to take advantage of you later. During a date rape, you have two enemies—the rapist, and the alcohol or drugs you have consumed.

Complicated Prosecution

There are many people, some of them unfortunately in law enforcement and the legal profession, who still believe that if you drink alcohol with someone and he ends up raping you, you asked for it. This is not true of course, but it has been a prevalent attitude. However, many people in law enforcement and the legal profession are starting to come around, finally changing their attitudes about blaming the victim for the rape.

Even if you drank to excess, you must remember that no one, no sane person, ever asks to be raped. There is only one person who is responsible for the crime of rape, and that is the rapist.

. . . .

Reality Check:
Blaming the rape victim serves only to sanction rape as a justifiable form of male behavior.

. . . .

Rape is the only crime for which society tends to blame the victim, and this is especially true when it comes to date and acquaintance rape. It is impossible to overstate the lack of sensitivity you may get from some men and women in law enforcement and in the courts if you had been drinking or taking drugs prior to the rape. They simply may not believe you or be willing to prosecute.

In one small town in Michigan, a college girl was raped by her date. The college believed her, but a local district attorney refused to prosecute because she had consumed one drink with the man three hours earlier. Unfortunately, the only way to avoid this problem is to abstain from drinking completely. If you have any sense that you may be in danger, consider refusing alcohol.

Even if you are dealing with sympathetic law enforcement officers, alcohol consumption may make it more difficult for you to remember what happened. You may even have become unconscious or blacked out. It is not uncommon for a woman to wake up after an assault with a sensation or feeling that something has happened to her, even though she does not remember the details. If you should ever awaken with a sense that you've been physically violated—but you cannot remember the incident—go to a rape crisis center or medical facility immediately for a medical exam.

The Rape Myth

Alcohol gives some men the idea that you can be manipulated and controlled if only they can get you drunk enough. Remember one of the most romantic scenes in the movie *Gone with the Wind,* where Rhett Butler has been drinking, supposedly because his wife Scarlet is in love with another man. When he sees her, he threatens to tear her head off. She rebukes him and starts for the stairs. He runs over to her, grabs her against her will, and carries her up the long sweeping staircase, saying that this is one night she won't lock him out of her room. The next morning, Scarlet wakes up with a glowing smile on her face. Rhett, however, shows no caring or concern for her and announces that he intends to leave for London. This scene also illustrates the fact that alcohol is often used by men to give them the courage to do what their consciences would normally prohibit.

Rape? I know it sounds as though I just destroyed a great American classic. But we are led to believe in this scenario that the man raped a woman, and she enjoyed it. Notice how it was alcohol that allowed Rhett Butler to overcome his inhibitions and get what he wanted. Perhaps you are saying that they were married—doesn't that make it acceptable? Absolutely not! This kind of scenario is all too common in many films and stories.

The myth is that it is acceptable for a man to use force to get a woman into bed. She will resist a little, and then she will just relax and enjoy it. There is an idea on the part of some men that all women want to be taken. If a young man were raped against his will by another man, it would increase his awareness of the agony and horror of rape.

Some men still believe that women want to be raped, perhaps not consciously, but in their subconscious. They think that a woman wants to be overpowered and subdued. It is true that some people do have fantasies about being overpowered by someone who is strong, confident, and self-assured, but that is nothing more than a very human desire at times to have someone else take control. It is only a fantasy, and it has nothing to do with the reality of rape. No one in her right mind ever wants or asks to be raped.

Even within a marriage, if the woman does not want sex and
the man forces it on her, that is rape.

· ·

Once, when discussing the writing of this book in a social setting, one man's immediate concern—and this is more common than you might think—was, "What about the girl who teases a guy and gets him all turned on and then changes her mind? What about the girl who has sex with him and then the next morning decides to get even with the guy by claiming she was raped?" This statement that some men and women invariably bring up is, in my opinion, a learned defense mechanism against giving women power. It is apparent that many men do not want to take real responsibility for their own sexual behavior. For a man, or for anyone else, to say that a woman invents being raped to get even with someone shows how little the person knows of the trauma, humiliation, and horror for the rape victim. Unsubstantiated charges of rape would appear to be a minuscule number in comparison with the actual rapes that are reported, especially considering that most rapes are never reported. According to the FBI, only 8 percent of violent crimes reported (including rapes) have been found to be unsubstantiated reports.[9]

Twenty years ago, alcohol was the most dangerous enabler in date rape crimes. Drugs, although dangerous and deadly, were not as easily obtainable, whereas alcohol was cheap and in plentiful supply. Today, alcohol is still the largest contributor to an acquaintance rape situation, but drugs are becoming more common and more problematic. Drugs such as marijuana, cocaine, and other chemicals have some of the same abilities as alcohol to increase confusion and reduce a woman's ability to resist her attacker. In 1996, the U.S. Congress passed a federal law increasing the penalties up to twenty years in prison for possession of a controlled substance with intent to commit a violent crime. What this amounts to is that a man using a drug to facilitate a rape may face federal penalties as well as state sanctions.

There are three commonly used narcotics on the scene, all of which cause a loss of muscle control and consciousness that are a danger to women and men, especially if they are administered to them without their knowledge (i.e., in a spiked drink).

What Are Date Rape Drugs?

These are drugs that are sometimes used to assist a sexual assault. It can include inappropriate touching, vaginal penetration, sexual intercourse, rape, and attempted rape. Because of the effects of these drugs, victims may be physically helpless, be unable to refuse sex, and be unable to remember what happened. The drugs often have no color, smell, or taste, and they are easily added to flavored drinks without the victim's knowledge. There are at least three rape drugs:

GHB (gamma hydroxybutyric acid)
Rohypnol (flunitrazepam)
Ketamine (ketamine hydrochloride)

Although we use the term "date rape," most experts prefer the term "drug-facilitated sexual assault." These drugs have been used to help people commit other crimes, such as robbery and physical assault, and they have been used on both men and women.

What Do the Drugs Look Like?

GHB has a few forms: a liquid with no odor or color, white powder, and pill.
Rohypnol is a pill and dissolves in liquids. New pills turn blue when added to liquids. However, the old pills, with no color, are still available.
Ketamine is a white powder.

What Effects Do These Drugs Have on the Body?

The drugs can affect you quickly. The length of time that the effects last varies. It depends on how much of the drug is taken and whether the drug is mixed with other substances, such as alcohol. Alcohol can worsen the drug's effects, and it can cause more health problems. Also, one drug—GHB—can be made by people in their homes, so you don't know what's in it.

GHB (Gamma Hydroxybutyric acid)
Liquid Extasy, Grievous Bodily Harms

GHB is often called "Liquid Extasy" because it comes in small bottles, with a capful of GHB providing users with X-like desires to be "touchy-feely," but its overall impact is likened more to that of LSD than Extasy. This makes sense because GHB is a psychedelic sleep-inducer, whereas X is an amphetamine. GHB is a powerful sedative that can leave the body limp and tired. X is frequently taken along with GHB to counteract this sedation.

GHB can cause these problems:
- relaxation
- drowsiness
- dizziness
- nausea
- problems seeing
- unconsciousness (blackout)
- seizures
- inability to remember what happened while drugged
- problems breathing
- tremors
- sweating
- vomiting
- slow heart rate
- dream-like feeling
- coma
- death

Rohypnol (Flunitrazepam)
Rophies, Ruffies, Roofies, La Rocha, Roofenal, Roche, R2, Mexican Valium, Rib, Rope

Rohypnol is a powerful sedative commonly prescribed as a sleeping pill in Europe and Latin America since 1975. It is illegal in the United States. The tablets manufactured in Mexico (the source for most of the U.S. supply) are round, white, and slightly smaller than an aspirin. The manufacturer's markings are similar to those found on other pills, including Rivotril and Valium.

The drug causes drowsiness, loss of inhibition and judgment, dizziness, confusion, and, in cases of high dosage, amnesia. "The drug's effects can begin within minutes," said Ann Marie Anglin, a spokesperson for Hoffmann-La Roche, the manufacturer of Rohypnol. Also, the drug's effects are intensified when used in conjunction with alcohol. Because it is sold in a bubble pack, it can be mistaken for a legal substance. Continued use can result in addiction.

Rohypnol can cause these problems:
• inability to remember what happened while drugged
• lower blood pressure
• sleepiness
• muscle relaxation or loss of muscle control
• drunk feeling
• nausea
• problems talking
• difficulty with motor movements
• loss of consciousness
• confusion
• problems seeing
• dizziness
• confusion
• stomach problems

Ketamine
Special K, Ketalar, Ketaject, Super-K

Ketamine has also been used in date rape situations, causing the victim to become detached, confused, and uncoordinated. Clear thinking and communication are both impaired under the influence of this drug. Ketamine is closely related to PCP, and it produces very similar effects. Like PCP, Ketamine use produces a reaction called a dissociative state, and, also like PCP, Ketamine is known to cause bad reactions in some of its users. However, unlike PCP, Special K is a legal prescription drug intended for use as an anesthetic for people and large animals. In recent years, Ketamine has begun to be used recreationally. Mixing this drug with alcohol is very dangerous.

Ketamine can cause these problems:
- hallucinations
- lost sense of time and identity
- distorted perceptions of sight and sound
- feeling out of control
- impaired motor function
- problems breathing
- convulsions
- vomiting
- out of body experiences
- memory problems
- dream-like feeling
- numbness
- loss of coordination
- aggressive or violent behavior
- slurred speech

Are These Drugs Legal in the United States?

Some of these drugs are legal, but that doesn't mean they're not going to hurt you. Even if they're legal, you should not use them unless your health care provider prescribes them.

Rohypnol is not legal in the United States. It is legal in Europe and Mexico, where it is prescribed for sleep problems and as an anesthetic (medicine given during surgery so you don't feel pain). It is brought into the United States illegally.

Ketamine is legal in the United States for use as an anesthetic for humans and animals. It is used mostly on animals. Veterinary clinics are robbed for their Ketamine supply.

GHB was recently made legal in the United States to treat problems related to narcolepsy (a sleep problem).

Is Alcohol a Date Rape Drug?

Although GHB, rohypnol, and ketamine are considered date rape drugs, there are other drugs that affect judgment and behavior, and they can put a person at risk for unwanted or risky sexual activity. Alcohol is one of those drugs.

When a person is drinking alcohol

- It's harder to think clearly and evaluate a potentially dangerous situation.
- It's harder to resist sexual or physical assault.
- Drinking too much alcohol can also cause blackouts and memory loss.

But remember, even if a victim of sexual assault drank alcohol, she is not at fault for being assaulted.

How Can I Protect Myself from Being a Victim?

- Don't accept drinks from other people.
- Open containers yourself.
- Keep your drink with you at all times, even when you go to the bathroom.
- Don't share drinks.
- Don't drink from punch bowls or other large, common, open containers. They may already have drugs in them.
- Don't drink anything that tastes or smells strange. Sometimes, GHB tastes salty.
- Have a nondrinking friend with you to make sure nothing happens.

If you think that you have been drugged and raped

- Go to the police station or hospital right away.
- Get a urine test as soon as possible. The drugs leave your system quickly. Rohypnol stays in the body for several hours, and it can be detected in the urine up to seventy-two hours after a person takes it. GHB leaves the body in twelve hours.
- Don't urinate before getting help.
- Don't douche, bathe, or change clothes before getting help. Doing any of these things may obscure or destroy evidence of the rape.
- You can also call a crisis center or a hotline to talk with a counselor. One national hotline is the National Sexual Assault Hotline at 1-800-656-HOPE (4673). Feelings of shame, guilt, fear, and shock are normal. It is important to get counseling from a trusted professional.

Date Rape Drug Myths:

Progesterex

Progesterex is a fictitious date rape drug. It is part of a hoax that began to circulate in 1999 via email. According to the U.S. Food and Drug Administration, the Center for Veterinary Medicine, the American Veterinary Medical Association, and Cornell University Equine and Farm Animal Hospital, no actual drug by this name or even with these properties exists, and no such incident has ever been documented or confirmed.

For more information on date rape drugs, contact the National Women's Health Information Center at 800-994-9662 or the following organizations:

Drug Enforcement Administration, DOJ
Phone: (202) 307-1000
Internet Address: http://www.usdoj.gov/dea

Food and Drug Administration, OPHS, HHS
Phone: (800) 332-4010 Hotline or (888) 463-6332 (Consumer
    Information)
Internet Address: http://www.fda.gov

National Institute on Drug Abuse, NIH, HHS
Phone: (800) 662-4357 Hotline or (800) 662-9832 Spanish Language
    Hotline
Internet Address: http://www.drugabuse.gov

Office of National Drug Control Policy
Phone: (800) 666-3332 (Information Clearinghouse)
Internet Address: http://www.whitehousedrugpolicy.gov/index.html

Men Can Stop Rape
Phone: (202) 265-6530
Internet Address: http://www.mencanstoprape.org

National Center for Victims of Crime
Phone: (800) 394-2255
Internet Address: http://www.ncvc.org

Rape, Abuse, and Incest National Network
Phone: (800) 656-4673 (656-HOPE)
Internet Address: http://www.rainn.org

Chapter Seven

The Four Personalities of the Rapist

Before you accept any generic crime prevention or self-defense advice, you should remember that there are three factors that will determine your ability to escape an attacker.

First, your response to the assault depends on your personality. You can be successful only if your response is practical. By that I mean that if you are told to scream, kick, fight, and act very aggressively, it will work only if your personality is not passive and shy. Conversely, if you are assertive and bold by nature, acting passive may not be possible for you. Your response will be more effective if it matches your personality.

Second, your response needs to be practical in terms of location. For example, screaming will be a waste of time in an isolated spot where no one can hear you but can work in public environment where others are likely to hear the noise. Some locations can actually give you an advantage. For example, a parking lot can give you the opportunity to crawl under a parked car.

The third and probably most important factor is this: Your response needs to take into consideration the personality type of the perpetrator. We as a society have a hard time thinking of attractive people as being dangerous. We have been conditioned by the media to think of rapists and other violent criminals as twisted, evil degenerates who are always repulsive and obnoxious. They are never like us or like the guy next door.

We know that not all rapists are alike. They operate differently, and they are motivated by different factors. The goal for the rapist is the thrill he gets by controlling and conquering his victim. Rapists seem to lack a sense of inner power. They may have a great deal of rage at all women, and that may be triggered by an incident with a specific woman from the past.

According to the FBI Behavioral Sciences Unit and many other experts in criminal psychology, there are four different types of personalities in men who commit rape. It is important that women understand that these are general patterns that may not apply to any one particular individual. The following illustration will indicate who the most common rapists are and who is getting all of the media attention.

Diagram 2: Four Personality Types of Rapists

POTENTIAL FOR VIOLENCE	
Gentleman Rapist Power, Reassurance	**Control Freak Rapist** Power, Assertive
Revenge Rapist Anger, Rotaliatory	**Sexual Sadist Rapist** Anger, Excitative

Gentleman Rapist (Power Reassurance)

The vast majority, 70 percent, of reported rapes are committed by men with Power Reassurance personalities. This kind of person is the most common type of date/acquaintance rapist and is often called the "Gentleman Rapist" because of his "gentlemanly" behavior after the rape. As the name indicates, the Power Reassurance rapist is less violent and less sure of himself. He seeks power and gets it through sex, or rape. He rarely carries a weapon, and he will often use coercion or the threat of violence to get control of his intended sexual partner. He doesn't consider his own behavior to be rape, and he will be shocked when he learns that he has been accused of rape. He believes in a fantasy of the encounter, actually thinking that he and the victim have just had a good time together. He will offer to drive or walk his victim home after the crime, and he will express concern for her safety. He most often will expect his victim to continue the "relationship" that he has started, and he may ask her out again the following night.

Robin Warshaw writes in *I Never Called it Rape*:

"Some acquaintance rapists become oddly tender immediately afterward and try to dress the woman or cover them [sic]. Some gallantly insist on walking or driving their victim home, telling the woman that it's dangerous for them to be out alone. Others profess love and talk about having an ongoing relationship. Another type kisses their victims good-bye and says they will call them again soon. (And some do call, apparently raring to go on another 'date.') In short, many men fail to perceive what has just happened as rape."

The Power Reassurance rapist may fantasize about having a relationship with his victim long before he gets her alone and will be planning to have sex with her very early in the relationship. He is the classic date rapist. Because he rarely uses a weapon, and doesn't generally inflict additional physical injury on his victim, he often will get the sympathy of those who know him. His mild manner on the surface, however, hides rage and a determination to get what he wants. He can cross over to become a Revenge Rapist or a Sexual Sadist and is just as dangerous, perhaps even more so, because he will most likely get away with his crime and do it again.

The man who commits date/acquaintance rape tends to be more selective in his victims and is more influenced by social standards of beauty—his victim is usually someone whom he would normally wish to date. He will often believe that he is being a man and that taking a woman by force is his right, an attitude that society seems to reinforce. The history of the media in this country is filled with movies, books, magazines, stories, television, and music videos that either condone or promote violence and rape. As mentioned earlier, even a classic such as *Gone with the Wind* may promote the traditional idea that men have the right of conquest over women and that after the assault a woman will thank the man and then reward him with her love. Although the motion picture and television industries have come a long way in terms of rape/violence messages, today's music and music videos are among the most violent and contain the most virulent antifemale messages that have ever been seen or heard. These media messages reinforce attitudes toward women that may cause some men to commit rape.

Prevention: As the most common of all rapists, and often the most respectable in society's eyes, this personality type is seldom seen as a criminal. The best way to break through to escape is to be assertive with him. You must make him understand that what he's about to do is not love, not sex, but rape! Attempt to break through his fantasy by screaming, fighting, or otherwise actively resisting him. Try to make him understand that what he is doing is a crime.

Control Freak (Power Assertive)

In 25 percent of all rape reports, the control freak personality surfaces. This personality tends to be found in a white male in his mid twenties with a blue collar job, who has the freedom to travel. This kind of rapist is more violent than the Gentleman Rapist, and he may initiate a sudden attack. He may carry a weapon, and he doesn't care about his victim. He will tend to be cruel to others and domineering in his attitude, often insisting that others do things his way. He may insist on ordering for a woman in a restaurant, and he will discourage her from having ideas and opinions of her own. He has often been called the "Dr. Jeckyl and Mr. Hyde" rapist because he may suddenly change in personality and appearance if he becomes threatened. His level of violence can escalate, and his personality can become that of the Revenge Rapist or Sexual Sadist at any time. This personality is generally the easiest to identify prior to the attack. He will often reveal his true personality early on in the relationship. His tendency is not to see a woman as a real person, and he will talk about women derisively and in a way that objectifies them.

Prevention: Talk to him, getting eye contact and making yourself real to him. There have been more than a few cases of rapists changing their minds when their victims were able to make a connection with someone that the rapist really cared about, such as a sister or mother. Talk about yourself and try to make him see you as a unique and real person.

Revenge Rapist (Anger Retaliatory)

Although only 4 percent of reported rapes can be traced to this personality type, it gets a lot of media attention. As the label indicates, there is anger here, and this man is retaliating against women. Usually a white male in his early thirties, he tends to be educated and somewhat successful, which enables him to travel extensively, making capture more difficult. This personality type may strike quickly with a high level of violence. Generally, there is a precipitating event that triggers rage, such as in the David Berkowitz case (the "Son of Sam"), where the rapist's rage was apparently triggered by family quarrels. This type of rapist's victims tend to be similar. He often takes a possession, or "trophy," from his victims. Although he may not originally intend to kill, he often does.

Prevention: You are in great danger when confronted by this type of rapist. This man harbors a great deal of hatred and rage. Your best bet is to attempt to escape, fighting with all your might, and trying not to let him get you to an isolated spot.

Sexual Sadist (Anger Excitative)

Only 1 percent of all reported rapists fall into this category, and these tend to be stranger-to-stranger rapes, or an acquaintance rape in which the victim and perpetrator had only just met. The very term indicates that this individual is angry and gets excited by the thrill of the crime. He intends to kill his victim. He will plan extensively, and he counts on the intended victim to provide him with an opportunity. He tends to be a white male in his thirties or forties, and he is generally well educated.

Ted Bundy falls into the category of a sexual sadist. His Volkswagen Beetle was always prepared for a kidnapping, with the right side-passenger seat removed and a tire iron stored in the back. He also carried around duct tape and handcuffs. Bundy's modus operandi was to lure victims to him by pretending he was helpless. He often wore a cast on his leg or arm. He was so good-looking that, when he asked a young female to help him with a box that he was struggling with, he would invariably get her to drop her guard and get close. Ted Bundy counted on his intended victims to be vulnerable and trust him. It is believed that he was responsible for killing more than thirty young girls and women.

Denial is so rampant among rape victims that, even when the facts are presented, many women can't bring themselves to believe that an attractive man can rape. During Bundy's trial, several women attended the proceedings wanting to have a relationship with him. As sick as it sounds, even up to his death, some of these women wanted him to be their friend, lover, or mate.

Prevention: If you are attacked by this kind of person, you can bet that you will have to fight like hell to get away. Because this type of individual is very clever, your best bet is to be aware and trust that inner guidance that tells you not to get too close or be alone with him. If you carry some kind of weapon, you must be prepared to use it at a moment's notice.

· ·

Reality Check:
Remember that some experts believe that all rapists are, in reality, serial rapists. That is, (according to Dr. Peg Ziegler) they rape repeatedly until stopped.

· ·

Rapists rarely stop themselves. The vast majority of rapists have access to sex, and what they're really after is not sex, but power. They tend to have a low sense of self-esteem, and this is their way of being powerful. They may have an addiction to the feelings of power and excitement that they experience from committing their crimes.

The real issue in rape prevention education is the increasing prevalence of some mens's rage. These men may think that their power base is being eroded by women, and some men may strike back at women in general by attacking particular women.

It is important to understand that rapists seldom fit neatly into one category or another. Often, they have traits from more than one personality type. A rapist can also progress by degrees from one category to another. In some cases, the rapist will get increasingly violent as his crimes continue because the excitement of the rape dissipates and he increases the violence to add to the excitement.

What Turns an Ordinary Man into a Rapist?

What turns an ordinary man into a date/acquaintance rapist? In many cases, it's a simple case of opportunity. If the opportunity exists, and the man thinks he won't get caught, he'll take it. In fact, a recent study by a major university indicated that a very alarming percentage of college and high school males would rape if they thought no one would ever find out.[12] Although this book is an attempt to get women to be alert to the potential dangers in dating as well as in all social situations, it is also a "cry in the wilderness" for men to stop their rage against women. For some people, the assumption is that if women would change their behavior, men might stop raping. That is not the case. If a woman changes her behavior and becomes more alert to the dangers around her, the best she can hope for is that the attacker will choose another victim. No matter what women do, some men will continue to rape.

The fact is that whether a woman is raped by a stranger or by someone she knows, she has still been violated. The pain is the same, the hurt is the same, and the feeling of having her innocence stripped away is the same. The trauma can be more intense when a woman is raped by her date/acquaintance or "friend," because she had an unspoken bond of trust with him. She knows strangers are dangerous, but when friends, dates, lovers, or husbands become rapists, whom can she trust? Who is her enemy?

Until men are reeducated about a women's right to her own body and sexual activities, this problem will continue. Education, unfortunately, takes time. For now, teens and women have to be alert, aware, and conscious that they can become targets of a man's violence.

It's All about Power

Why do men rape? And why do they rape women they know? Society has misunderstood the method and modality of the rapist. We think we can understand a young attractive woman being raped, but not a child, and not an older woman. Not until we understand that rape is about power will we understand the rape or the rapist. Date rape or acquaintance rape is a violent act of control perpetrated, not by a sick inhuman animal, but by an average guy who, given the right circumstances and the right frame of mind, may commit rape. It may even be that he would never consider himself a rapist.

In general, if you ask a man if he has ever raped a woman, he will of course say that he has not. But, ask him again whether he has ever had sex with someone against her will, when he knew that she did not want to participate. You will be amazed at the number of men who will say that indeed they have had sex under such circumstances. In addition, a man's behavior may change with the situation. Although it may appear to the victim to be a spontaneous act, often an acquaintance rape is not at all spontaneous. In some cases, plans are made, and people or potential witnesses are gotten rid of to make the situation safe for the rapist and unsafe for the intended victim.

....

Reality Check:
When you are confronted with a man who intends to
rape you, you must assume the very worst
in order for you to respond effectively.

....

However well you may have thought you knew this man, he is now your enemy, and your life is in danger. Follow your instincts and quickly act to protect yourself. Remember, if you escape, or even if you just survive, then you did the right thing.

Stranger Rape

Stranger rape is primarily an act of violence to control, in which the attacker attempts to humiliate and degrade the victim. The purpose of this kind of rape is to gain power through intimidation. In *The Gift of Fear*, Gavin de Becker outlines the conclusions of his research on the techniques that criminals often use to prey upon women. These techniques are similar to, but different in degree from, the warning signs that a date rapist might exhibit. If you observe a man using one or more of these techniques, you should be on your guard and get away from him quickly. Do not allow yourself to be alone with him, and do not hesitate or analyze. Act quickly to protect yourself.

Criminal Techniques

Forced Teaming: This is a tactic of manipulation in which the man attempts to create a shared purpose or experience where none exists. The man refers to the woman and himself as "we," even if they have just met, and even when it is highly inappropriate, and he attempts to make the woman feel that he and she are sharing a common pursuit or purpose.

Prevention: When you notice this kind of behavior, ask yourself, "Why is he trying to create a team of the two of us?" Remind yourself that you and he are not sharing an experience, and remain on your guard.

Charm and Niceness: "To charm is to compel or control by allure or attraction," says de Becker. Rather than thinking that a man is charming, a woman should say to herself, "This man is trying to charm me." Many women who have been assaulted report that the man was extremely "nice" at the beginning. Beware of behavior that is seems excessive, inappropriate, or dazzling.

Prevention: If you have a sense that a man is exhibiting behavior that is unusual for the situation, ask yourself, "Why might he be acting so nicely?" or, "Why would he be trying to charm me?"

Too Many Details: It is common for a person who is lying to offer too many details in an effort to bolster his credibility. A person who is telling the truth is not preoccupied with whether or not he is being believed, whereas a person who is lying will work hard to be convincing.

Prevention: If you are hearing a mass of details or background information that you did not solicit, you should ask yourself, "Why is he trying to convince me?" Try not to get too distracted by the story so that you can remain alert and clear about what is really going on.

Typecasting: A common maneuver is to make a slightly critical statement that challenges the listener to prove the opposite. The man does not necessarily believe what he is saying; he believes only that his statement will affect the woman's behavior. For example he might say, "You're so well dressed that you're probably really uptight and wouldn't know how to have a good time." The woman may find herself trying to prove to him that she does know how to have a good time, and she may go along with things she otherwise wouldn't in order to not be perceived as "uptight."

Prevention: The best way to counteract this tactic is to say nothing and not to take the bait. If you find yourself thinking, "I'll show him I'm not uptight," you are falling into his trap.

Any one of the above maneuvers may be used to attempt to control or manipulate a woman into a situation in which the assailant has power over her. Power is so much the focus of the exercise that, in a stranger rape situation, copulation often is not completed. The turn-on for the rapist is the conquest of power, not sex. This sometimes escalates into further and further acts of violence against the victim. Stranger rape can be compared to an addict's drug habit. As his addiction increases, his need also increases for more drugs (or, in this case, for more violence) to achieve the same high. Some rapists need to hurt their victims a little more with each assault until the only thing that gives them their high is to kill.

This kind of criminal may eventually become obsessed with the thrill of killing his victim and will increase the frequency of his crime until he is caught or stopped. He does not, in many cases, wait for the right circumstances to commit his crime, and he will often go to great lengths to create the ideal situation. To this kind of criminal, age, race, sex, or physical characteristics mean nothing.

Gang Rape

According to the U.S. Department of Justice, gang rape accounts for about 9 percent of all reported rapes.[13] However, the physical and emotional damage that is inflicted upon the victim of a gang rape is enormous. In *Against Our Will*, Susan Brownmiller writes: "When men rape in pairs or gangs, the sheer physical advantage of their position is clear-cut and unquestionable. No simple conquest of man over woman, group rape is the conquest of men over woman."

Often, individual men who commit gang rape would normally be too timid to perpetrate a rape by themselves; however when they become part of a group of men, this changes, particularly if there has been a great deal of alcohol consumed. Men who commit gang rape experience a special bonding, and there seems to be a sense of pride in humiliating their victim. There is a perception that they are proving their manhood and improving their standing within the group if they participate in the rape. Generally, the group leader is the first to commit rape, and the others will then follow. It is also true that part of the motivation for the members of the gang is to not lose status or look bad in front of the others.

Gang rape is generally much more violent and abusive than normal date and acquaintance rape. The perpetrators of gang rape appear to have a lot of hostility and rage against women and, if prosecuted, they may go to great lengths to deny the incident and accuse the victim. Gang rapes are more common at events where alcohol and drugs are consumed. Fraternity parties and athletic parties can be a breeding ground for this kind of assault.

Prevention: If all else fails, and you find yourself being assaulted by a group of men, try to make eye contact with one person. Tell him to go get help. That way you may be able to break the male bonding and make him feel compassion for you. Depending on his personality and the group's control over him, it may or may not work. What you are doing here is trying to make a personal connection with just one rapist. If you can get him to see you as a person and not a "thing" to be used, then maybe he will have the courage to help you. Above all, remember that, regardless of the circumstances, the attack is not your fault.

Chapter Eight

The ABCs of Date Rape

There are three factors that make up the ABCs of date and acquaintance rape. They are Agenda, Belief, and Communication. Not all acquaintance rapes are preplanned acts of violence. All rapes constitute violence, but many start as miscommunication and faulty belief systems that add to the problem of understanding the opposite sex.

In Chapter Four, I discussed the date rape triangle, the three factors that exist at the time of almost all sexual assaults taking place in a dating situation. In this chapter, I want to discuss the broader social context as it applies to date rape, and as I have interpreted it from hundreds of conversations with attendees at my Rape Prevention seminars. The topics in this chapter are broad in scope and are the realm of sociologists, who have many different views on societal shifts. It is important for women, however, to take into consideration the context in which their dating experiences are occurring. Such awareness decreases a woman's vulnerability. It also may allow an individual woman to see more clearly how an individual man might pose a potential danger to her, and to take the necessary steps to protect herself.

First of all, it must be seen that, in spite of many advances for women over the past few decades, women are still pervasively discriminated against and experience inequity in many areas of life. There is a great deal of ambivalence throughout our society about gender roles and differences. Many women who view themselves as equals to men run into men who resist this view. Boys and girls are still raised with markedly different attitudes, resulting in apparent "innate" differences in adult men and women. The popularity of such books as *Men Are from Mars, Women Are from Venus* by John Gray and *You Just Don't Understand* by Deborah Tannen attest to the widely held notion that there may be fundamental differences in men and women. Many women's advocates object to the notion that there are inherent gender differences because, for so many years, these differences have been cited as a way to justify gender discrimination. Yet many mothers will tell you that their sons and daughters appear to come into the world with different predilections and inborn interests.

At the very least, it is fair to say that certain aspects that may be present in all people are emphasized in people's upbringing, depending on their gender. For example, whereas all people may be inclined toward independence and competitiveness to some degree, these qualities are encouraged in boys, and although all people need cooperation and relatedness, these are emphasized in girls. When these boys and girls grow up to be adults and begin to seek each other out both romantically and sexually, there may be marked differences in their agendas, belief systems, and communication modes. The clash of these elements may result in date rape.

Again, while it is ultimately up to men to stop all rape—and I encourage men to grapple with the ABCs of date and acquaintance rape—I believe it is imperative for a woman to ascertain the agenda of her date, to explore his belief system, to look for the qualities that many rapists share, and to use the most effective communication she can to remain safe from sexual assault.

A=Agenda

Men's Agenda

Many men have a different agenda from women in relationships.

If men and women both wanted the same things in a relationship, there would be far less miscommunication. However, this is usually not the case. When a man is in his early years, from age seventeen to twenty-five, he may be preoccupied with sex—it may be on his mind constantly.

A man may think that women exist for only one reason—to have sex with him. This time in his life may be filled with doubts about his own masculinity, frustration, fear, and a strong need to be accepted by his peers. He may feel that the only way to prove his manhood to himself and his peers is by having sex. Locker-room talk reflects this need on the part of young men to prove their importance through sexual conquest.

Reality Check:
Sex, or the ability to have sex with a woman, should have nothing to do with a secure, healthy man's sense of self-worth.

Erik Johnke, a male student at Haverford College, described the gender role-playing that goes on between a man and a woman on a date. The following is taken from his senior thesis as quoted in *I Never Called it Rape* by Robin Warshaw.

"The man is taught to look upon his actions on a date as a carefully constructed strategy for gaining the most territory. Every action is evaluated in terms of the final goal—intercourse. He continually pushes to see 'how far he can get.'"

"Every time she (his date) submits to his will, he has 'advanced,' and every time she does not, he has suffered a 'retreat.' Since he already sees her as the opponent, and the date as a game or a battle, he anticipates resistance."

"He knows that 'good girls don't,' and so she will probably say 'no,' but he has learned to separate himself from her and her interests. He is more concerned with winning the game. Instead of trying to communicate with her, he attempts to pressure her into saying 'yes.'"

"Every time she submits to his will, he sees it as a small victory (getting the date, buying her a drink, getting a kiss, or fondling her breasts). He plays upon her indecisiveness, using it as an opportunity to tell her 'what she really wants,' which is, in fact, what he wants. If her behavior is inconsistent, he tells her that she is 'fickle' or 'a tease.' If he is disinterested in her desires and believes that she is inconsistent, he is likely to ignore her even when she does express her desires directly. When she finally says, 'no,' he simply may not listen, or he may convince himself that she is just 'playing hard to get' and that she really means 'yes.' With such a miserable failure of communication, a man can rape a woman even when she is resisting vocally and physically, and still believe that it was not rape."

Women's Agenda

Women may want different things from relationships than men do—this is especially true in the early years. As men and women get older, they tend to become more alike and share the same wants, needs, and goals in their relationships and lives. But in the teenage and early adult years—ages sixteen to thirty—they can be separated by vast differences. For women, relationships mean cooperation and support. They want companionship and friendship. They look for men who communicate and make them feel secure and safe. For them, communication is extremely important. They grow up sharing feelings, desires, dreams, and ambitions with their mothers and other females. When life is difficult, they get comfort and understanding through talking it out with a close friend. Men, when life gets difficult, may withdraw from communication.

Prevention: It is easy to see how this clash in agendas—men seeking sex, women seeking companionship—can lead to disastrous results. The safest thing for a woman in a younger age bracket is to assume that a man she's dating has sex on his agenda and make her decisions accordingly. More mature women may be able to draw their conclusions after some communication has taken place. Although it may seem like an awkward thing to do, a woman would do well to discuss her own agenda for the date right at the outset of the evening.

B=Beliefs
Men's Beliefs

Many men have very distinct beliefs about men and women. They often believe that most women are manipulative and controlling and that they generally don't know what they want. They are perplexed about women's emotional states most of the time, preferring logic to emotion, mainly because many men are trained from boyhood to express themselves through logic and to suppress their emotions. On the other hand, they want women's sexual favors. The old adage, "Men give love to get sex," is still true for many men. Many men who commit rape perceive women as sexual teases who change their minds after getting the man excited. These men tend to believe that once they become sexually aroused, they have to copulate and cannot stop until it's over. These men may be capable of completely separating the act of sex from the emotion of love, and may see women as objects whose purpose is to serve men.

Some men with these kinds of beliefs believe that a husband cannot rape his wife and that she is the property of her husband. They also may believe a man should be in strict control of finances and decisions in the home and that he is the head of the household. These beliefs are often reinforced by the world's major religions, which are based upon male dominance.

Fortunately, some men have been influenced by the women's movement and are beginning to view relationships as more equitable. This shift also may take place as a man reaches his thirties and forties and may begin to see the importance and appeal of a balanced relationship.

Women's Beliefs

Today, many women believe that all men want only one thing. This is especially true if they are young and going out with younger men. They tend to think that men are jerks, that they can't communicate, or that they won't share their feelings. They often don't feel that men are very smart, and they believe that men are certainly not sensitive and caring.

Some women also feel that men don't understand them, and they are perplexed by men's unwillingness to talk and share. They see men often in roles of control and manipulation and resent their attitudes about women in general. Many women who have attended my seminars can't understand why any man would rape or assault someone, because they are not driven for power as men are. In spite of all this, they love men and look for a loving, caring, and supportive partner with whom they can build a relationship. Most of these women see relationships as a "win-win" situation. They look for partners who will respect them and put time and work into the relationship. They are used to sharing their feelings and to experiencing enduring relationships with other females.

Many women need support and love and a feeling of safety before they give sexual favors. Emotional closeness is very important to them. The old adage, "A woman gives sex to get love," remains true for many women.

For many women, having sexual intercourse is the most intimate and vulnerable situation they can be in, so a feeling of safety and emotional support is vital. Such a woman has a hard time separating sex from her feelings about the man with whom she is involved. In essence, she needs to be loved and cherished and made to feel special before she feels comfortable having sexual contact.

Prevention: A woman must ascertain early on the extent to which the man she is dating believes that women are inferior to men. She must listen closely to his words and carefully observe his behavior. Remember that disparaging remarks about women along with inappropriately controlling behavior may be warning signals of a rapist.

C=Communication

Communication between men and women has become increasingly difficult as roles are in flux. Some men are confused today as to what women want and expect from them. Men and women may communicate differently, and for different reasons. It is beyond the scope of this book to argue whether this is learned or innate; it is just the reality with which we're dealing at this time. Date rape can start as a failure of communication.

Based on my experience with a wide range of people, for women, talk is the glue that holds relationships together, whereas for men, relationships are held together primarily by activities such as sports or politics. The situations in which men are most inclined to talk are those in which they feel the need to impress, in circumstances where their status is in question.

Whereas women communicate to get cooperation and consensus, men tend to communicate to establish position and hierarchy. Men in general have difficulty talking unless there is some definite point to make or information to obtain. Women, on the other hand, communicate with greater ease and establish friendships and nonhierarchical groups.

Dr. David Viscott, in his book *I Love You, Let's Work it Out*, comments on the miscommunication about affection that often happens between men and women:

"It is especially difficult for many men to understand that the warmth and friendship of just being together is as important as sex in the relationship. Without this closeness, most women feel cheated, unloved, and unwilling to be sexually involved, although they may have sex in the hope that there will be a tender moment afterward. Unfortunately, if the tender moment is not there before, it is unlikely that it will be there later."

"Affection is diminished when it is misread as an invitation for sex. Mostly it is men who misinterpret affectionate approaches. The woman, usually wanting closeness, with sex far removed from her mind, reaches out to be affectionate to her mate and finds him suddenly aroused, thinking she wants to make love. This disappoints and hurts her, and she pulls back. He accuses her of starting something that she won't finish."

At this point, the man—if he's aggressive and determined, and if he feels that his manhood has been abused—may use force to finish what he thinks the woman started in the first place.

In a relationship, people need to communicate to establish closeness and a feeling of caring for each other. Women's great complaint is that men don't communicate. This is not true—they do communicate, but when they do, it is often nonverbal communication. Many men show their feelings, not by words, but by deeds. If you want to communicate effectively with a man, do it in terms he's used to, not in words that he may not hear, but in actions.

Communication is much more than words. Only 7 percent of communication is verbal, whereas 38 percent is tone of voice, and 55 percent is body language. That means that in order to communicate effectively , a woman must use all three—words, tone of voice, and body language to get her point across. This is true especially if alcohol and drugs are being used.

Reality Check:

You have to use all three means of communication—
verbal, tone of voice, and body language—
when you are communicating with a man on a date.

. . . .

A major problem in acquaintance rape situations occurs when a woman sends mixed messages, either due to ambivalence, to a desire to be "nice," or for some other reason. If she is saying, "no," but her tone of voice is not reinforcing that she means what she says, the man may not get the message. And if she is saying, "no," but her body language is not saying the same thing, the man may instead believe what he wants to believe.

You may have spent the entire evening trying to tell your date that you were not interested in a sexual relationship, but he may not have heard you. He will, however, understand your message if you do something physical. The simple act of removing your hand from his will get his attention much faster than gently dropping a verbal hint in an ongoing conversation.

Communication through What You Wear

There is a lot of misinformation out there about the importance of what a woman wears in relation to her susceptibility to rape. In fact, figures indicate that a victim's choice of apparel contributed to the rapist's decision to commit rape in only 3 percent of all rape cases. Yet, we are a visual society, and people respond to what they see. Many men and women still believe that if a woman wears a provocative outfit, she's "asking for it." This is rarely the case! A woman may wear a provocative outfit to attract attention and be noticed, but attracting attention is not asking to be raped. If a man drives a flashy sports car, does that mean he's asking to be robbed? Of course not!

Reality Check:
No matter what a woman wears, it does not give a man
permission to molest, assault, or rape her.
It is inappropriate to blame men's criminal behavior
on the clothing worn by women.

What a woman wears does send messages, however, and if she is trying to be taken seriously and not as a sexual object, she needs to be conscious of the message she's sending. If you want to send a message to a man that says, "I am a woman who deserves to be treated with respect," then try sending the message visually through what you wear. Reinforce the visual message with words and actions. That way, you are more likely to communicate what you want, and he is more likely to get the message.

You should also understand that there are no guarantees; you may be dressed like a nun and still get raped.

So the key here is, wear what is comfortable, and be consistent and clear with the message you are trying to send to the world. You have the right to walk around wearing as little or as much as you wish. However, everything we do has consequences. Wearing clothing that sends mixed signals to men might make it much harder for you to convince them that you're not easy prey. Someday society will not blame women for rape based on what they wear, and men will not automatically assume that a provocative outfit means you are looking for sex, but until that day comes, be alert to the kind of messages you're sending—whether or not they're intentional—and to the kind of responses you're getting from others. If changing your wardrobe results in fewer problems with men, it might be worth the change.

The key in preventing date rape is to be consistent with all of the communication that you send. Your words, tone of voice, and body language should all be saying the same thing. That's effective communication. Great relationships are about effective and consistent communication. Start your relationship off right by saying what you mean. Silence can lead to misinformation and assumptions. Speak up. Speak clearly. Say what's on your mind, and keep saying it until you know you have reached him. He can't read your mind, so don't expect him to.

One way to establish your independence right away is to approach each dating situation on equal ground. Insist on having your own transportation and on paying your own expenses. Under these conditions, a woman is not as likely either to feel or be perceived to be obligated to a man. The man is also less likely to think that she owes him sexual favors because she spent her own money. This is especially a good idea when the parties do not know each other very well.

Seven Keys to Clear Communication

The clearer your communication is in a dating situation, the safer you are. Use the following seven techniques to protect yourself. (Understand that when you drink or take any kind of drugs, your ability to communicate clearly will be affected, both because your speech may become slurred and because you may not be focused enough to interpret signals that he is sending out that should be taken as true warnings.)

1. Speak forcefully and clearly! This is no time for a weak squeaky voice. Try lowering your voice, which makes it sound more authoritative.
2. Look him straight in the eye! We all have different ways of communicating and listening. Just saying the words without making eye contact may not be enough. Establishing eye contact is one way to assure yourself that he has heard what you said.
3. Make sure he has heard you and understood you. Simple is better. Get some kind of acknowledgment from him. If he mumbles, ask him, "Do you understand me?"
4. Make sure he understands that he is—and you are not—responsible for his actions. You will know whether what you've said has made an impact by judging his actions. If he becomes immediately defensive by saying he can't stop if he gets turned on, then you must be more assertive about what you want out of the date.
5. Make sure he understands that you and you alone will decide if and when you participate in any sexual activity. You do have power. Many men believe that women are the "gatekeepers" of men's sexual

pleasure. In reality, you hold the key to only your own sexual activity. He holds the key to his. You also can explain how much more fulfilling and wonderful the act of intercourse will be if both of you are ready and are in agreement about when to initiate sex into the relationship.

6. Let him know, in no uncertain terms, that failure to honor your wishes will result in severe consequences for him. Sometimes you have to go to extremes to communicate. Don't settle for something and someone you don't want. Do whatever it takes to get your point across. Don't get talked into going along to please him. He may say, "I love you. If you loved me you'd do it." You can always say, "If you really loved me, you wouldn't ask me to do something that I don't want to do."

7. Tell him, "After I say no, it's rape!" Non-consensual sex is rape, and sometimes you have to call it what it is. The vast majority of men to whom I've talked, who have admitted to having sex with a woman when she didn't want to, would never identify their own actions as rape. They deny that they could ever do such a thing. If you are saying "no," and you are not being heard, clearly state that you consider that he has no further right to touch or control you.

Specific Prevention Phrases

Following are some specific phrases or sentences you can use early in the evening, before any physical contact has taken place:

1. "I want you to know that I'm not interested in a physical relationship now, and I would appreciate it if you would honor my feelings and not pressure me at this point. Okay?"

2. "I would feel more comfortable if we met each other at [a neutral location]. Okay?"

3. "I want to drive my car because I feel safer that way. Please understand, this is no reflection on you. This is something I always do during the first few dates. Okay?"

4. "I don't appreciate your statement about women. I am a woman too and when you talk about women, you are talking about me. If you want my respect, you must treat all women with respect. Okay?"

5. "Is that a put down? If it is, I don't appreciate it. Please don't do that again. Okay?"

Do not be afraid to pin him down for his comments. If you sit there and take it and say nothing, he may either assume that you agree with him or that you are too weak to confront him and that you will say nothing later if and when he begins to rape you.

You will notice that in statements one to five, each statement is followed by you asking, "Okay?" There is a good reason for this. You are asking for his acknowledgment and agreement with your desires and wishes. You are not asking for his permission. You also really want to know if he has heard you. Some men often turn women off in their heads and do not really listen to their words. This is not necessarily done with malice or even consciously, but often they are self-absorbed and not used to listening to women. You must be sure that your communication has been heard and understood. Later in the evening, if his behavior is in conflict with his earlier agreement with your wishes, he can be reminded of his agreement. It is also the case that if he's drinking, he may not physically hear you, as people who drink can suffer some hearing loss.

6. "I'm feeling uncomfortable with your behavior. I want to go home. Please take me home right now."
7. "I'm going home. You don't have to drive me. I have my own car." [Or, "I am calling a friend to pick me up."]
8. "I don't feel like drinking. Please don't pressure me to drink when I don't want to."

You may indicate to him that you are not going to drink by turning your glass over or by telling the server that you will not be drinking tonight and asking that the wine glass be taken away. Involving the server is a good idea because you now have a witness that you did not drink or that you stopped drinking at some point in the evening.

I know that some of these techniques may sound extreme, especially in a dating situation, but it is better to sound strong and clear in your communication than to be silent or unclear and be perceived as weak and submissive.

Chapter Nine

What to Do If You Are Confronted

....

Reality Check:
There are no guarantees that rape will
not happen to you no matter how careful you are
and no matter how well-prepared you are.

....

Naturally, it is important to practice as much prevention as possible, and that includes moderation of alcohol consumption and watching for any signs or danger signals that a man may be giving.

Rape is an act of violence and control, not an act of sex, love, or seduction. Even if you lose control in a dating situation, you may be able to regain what you've lost by re-establishing a strong line of direct communication. If communication does not work to avert the assault, you may need to resort to fighting back.

Verbal Self-Defense

First of all, try to talk to your assailant, and be clear in your communication. The earlier—in a dating situation—your wishes are known to him, the more likely he will be to honor your desires or lack of desires for him. As the situation escalates, he may either not believe you or think you are playing hard to get.

Your words are only 7 percent of your communication; 38 percent is the tone of your voice, and 55 percent of your communication is in your body language. Your tone of voice and your body language must match your words.

A man is more likely to believe your body language, or his perceptions of your body language, than your words, especially if they are in conflict. Some men tend to believe that a woman doesn't know what she wants. If your communication is open to interpretation, the man may interpret it to his advantage and to your disadvantage.

If you are in a situation where you are alone with a man who is becoming sexually aggressive, you may succeed in averting the attack if you can

- Try to stop the momentum long enough for him to look at you.
- Try to get him to think about what he is doing and the consequences of his actions.
- Try to get him to think about you as a person, not as an "object" that he must control or has the right to conquer.

Remember that he may not be listening to you, so you need to communicate with strength and clarity. Make your statements strong.

You may try to lower your voice because a high voice can sound weak and too feminine for him to take you seriously. He may tend to listen to you more if your voice is harder and stronger.

The following statements are suggestions that may work for you. There is no one statement or group of words that will work in all situations. Every situation is different. Use your instincts. Listen to that inner voice and let it guide you on how you can best reach this guy, and act quickly.

If you do not wish to accept his more physical advances, you may find some of these statements effective (these are only suggestions; put them into your own words if they don't sound right for you):

"Back off! I need my space!"

"Stop touching me. I don't want you to do that. Stop it now!"

"What you are doing is making me uncomfortable. Please stop it right now!"

"What do you think you're doing?"

"Are you trying to get me drunk so that you can take advantage of me?" (This is no joke, so do not let him humor or patronize you by not taking you seriously.)

"Why are you trying to get me drunk? Remember our agreement—that I'm not going to bed with you tonight!"

If he continues to make physical overtures to you, and you feel you are entering the first stages of a sexual assault, you will need to increase the strength of your language:

"I know what you're trying to do. It's called rape!"

"I want you to know that if you continue, I will report you to campus security and the police department."

"Are you prepared for the consequences of your actions?"

"Are you prepared to be branded as a rapist by me and the police?"

"Are you prepared for what will happen to you if you continue this assault?

"You will lose your standing at the University."

"You will be known as a rapist."

"You will not be able to get a decent job, and there is every possibility that you will go to jail! Are you prepared for that? If so, then I'm warning you that I will fight you with all of my strength!"

"I will prosecute you to the fullest extent of the law."

"I will pursue you and inform everyone that I meet that you are a rapist, and, even if the authorities decide not to prosecute you, I can assure you that I will ruin you, if it's the last thing I do. Ten years from now, when you think you have forgotten me, I will remember you, and just when you think you will never hear from me again, I will be on your doorstep to inform your wife and your children that you are a rapist!"

Tell him you have a venereal disease or AIDS. Act crazy or as if you are on drugs and having a hallucination. Fighting back mentally may work just as well as physical action. Such maneuvers may make you too much for him to deal with.

These words may be uncomfortable for you just because you are saying things during a date that you normally would not say. You may be uncomfortable simply because you are not used to being assertive with him. The language may seem extreme, but it is meant to protect you from an attacker. You may have to pull out all the stops and be more aggressive than you've ever imagined.

You may fear that such assertiveness will put your relationship at risk, simply because he may not be able to handle a woman whom he cannot manipulate and control. Face facts. You may lose him, but think of the alternatives. If this guy is thinking of or planning to rape you, anything you can do or say that changes his plans is a victory for you. If he is so intimidated by your assertiveness that he drops you like a hot potato, then do you really want him in your life?

Remember, there are no guarantees. Anything can happen to you. While confrontational words will work with some rapists in some situations, they may make him more violent if his personality bristles at being confronted by a woman. As with all crime prevention maneuvers, you take your chances no matter what you do. If he starts to get more violent or abusive when you verbally confront him, back off! Listen to your inner guidance to know exactly what to do and how to avoid making the situation even more violent.

Physical Maneuvers

There is a difference between the amount of force that generally accompanies acquaintance rapes and the amount that occurs in stranger rapes. Stranger rapists are generally more violent. For the date rapist, the act of having sex is how he exerts his control, whereas the stranger rapist is more interested in controlling and gaining power over his victim than in having sex with her. This kind of rapist may resort to violence to exert his power over the woman and physically abuse her along with the actual rape.

Fifteen Maneuvers That May Work

The following physical maneuvers are considered effective by many people in stopping an attacker:

1. Kick him in the shins.
2. Slap his face.
3. Scratch his face.
4. Pull his hair.
5. Pull his little finger back to break it.
6. Kick him in the groin.
7. Pretend to faint.
8. Urinate, defecate, or vomit on him or on yourself.
9. Run from him.
10. Scream, "Help!" "Police!" "Rape!" or, "Fire!" Most experts believe you will get more response if you yell, "Fire!"
11. Make a loud noise or use a noise device.
12. Step on his foot, especially his instep, with your high heels.
13. Thumb to the eyeball push: When his guard is down, place your hands on each side of his face in a caressing motion. Move your hands toward the corners of his eyes and push your thumbs into the corners of his eyes. He will immediately go into shock, his eyes will pop out of his sockets, and you should then have the opportunity to escape.
14. Testicle jerk: In this maneuver, you pretend to go along with the rape and get yourself into a position where you are close to his penis. Sooner or later, he will expose himself. Once he does, take hold of the testicles and jerk as hard as you can. This will cause him immense pain. He should bend over holding his crotch, which should give you enough time to escape.
15. If all of the above fail or are not possible, appear to cooperate. He is not expecting this and may then drop his guard or his weapon, giving you an opportunity to escape.

The acquaintance rapist is less likely to use excessive force on his victims. The physical maneuvers that most people associate with repelling a rapist will probably be more effective on the date rapist than on the stranger rapist.

Whatever is happening, try to remain calm if you can. Breathe deeply. This will reduce the shock and get oxygen to your brain, which allows you to think more clearly. Keep your focus on distracting your attacker long enough for you to have an opportunity to escape.

Escape

Your primary objective is to escape your attacker. If you have an opportunity, you must take advantage of it instantly to get away from him. While you seek this opportunity, get as prepared as possible. If you are in high heels, take them off. You can't run in them. If you are not dressed for running, make whatever adjustments are necessary to get away. (Tight skirt? Get it up above your knees.) If it means that you have to run out of his place in your bare feet or partially clothed, don't hesitate. Move, and move fast! Run toward light and people, or get in a car and lock the doors and hit the horn until someone comes to your rescue. If you are in a parking garage or around a parked car, you can get down and crawl under the parked car—it will be hard for him to reach you there. (Scream "Fire" from under the car.)

Weapons

Many of the physical maneuvers listed above may not be effective during a stranger rape situation as there is generally less time to think. Stranger rapists are also more violence-prone and often use lethal weapons. These techniques are no match against a gun or knife.

Using some weapons yourself can be very effective in date rape situations because the date rapist is usually not armed and expects little to no resistance to his advances. It is important to be realistic, however, in choosing a weapon. Your boyfriend, father, or some other well-meaning man may quickly recommend carrying a gun, or even give you a gun. Think very carefully about whether you can use it without hesitation in an assault situation. You may think you can, but many women, faced with criminal assault, cannot effectively use a lethal weapon on an attacker, and they end up hesitating. This hesitation may allow the criminal to gain control, confiscate the weapon, and use it against his intended victim.

Many women in this situation are in such a state of shock when their date/acquaintance starts to rape them that they do not interpret his actions as rape. This misidentification of a violent crime may cause additional delay in using a lethal weapon. The intended victim also may not understand that what is about to occur is a crime.

Susan Estrich writes in *Real Rape*, "It appears that most women forced to have sex by men they know see themselves as victims, but not as legitimate crime victims."

If a woman doesn't consider herself a "legitimate crime victim," how could she justify using force to stop the crime? Another reason she may not respond is that it is more difficult for some women to inflict pain on another person.

Most women are not taught as children to act aggressively toward other people. They tend to be more concerned about not hurting another's feelings than men are. In fact some women are unfortunately more comfortable receiving pain than giving pain.

In many situations, a woman may find it so difficult to pull out the stops and injure her attacker that she either hesitates or does not do it at all. She also may be worried that she cannot hurt him enough to stop him so she would rather not risk provoking him further.

Reality Check:
Remember that there are no guarantees. Anything you do or don't do could make the situation better or worse.

No one can give you absolute advice as to how to handle a rape situation. Every situation is different. Remember once again that what works for one woman may not work for another. Every woman is different. Every rapist is different. Do what your inner guidance tells you to do.

Whatever you decided to do or to not do, don't be too hard on yourself.

Try not to blame yourself or judge yourself too harshly. Rape is a crime of violence and intimidation. If you escaped or survived, then you did exactly the right thing.

....

Reality Check:

Whatever decision you made in the past, or may make in the future, you did the best you could under the circumstances. Remember, if you make it through the assault alive, then you are not a victim. You are a survivor of a violent crime.

....

You can come though this situation and recover. You do not have to face it all alone.

There are many people—doctors, police officers, lawyers, therapists, ministers, friends, family, and support groups—who can be of great help. Don't try to handle it alone. Don't try to ignore what happened to you and just continue your life as if nothing happened. You have had a life-threatening situation happen to you. You may suffer from post-traumatic stress disorder, just like a battlefield soldier, even if you escaped before the rape took place. Attempted rape can be extremely traumatic.

Find people who understand and care. Search the internet. Consult the Yellow Pages. Talk to doctors, police, and therapists for referrals. Keep searching until you find the right therapist, support group, doctor, or minister, who knows what you're feeling and cares enough to help. Now that you are reading this book, you know there are many other women who have experienced what you have gone through.

You are not alone!

Chapter Ten

Weapons, Martial Arts, and Self-Defense Courses

No weapon or martial arts training is any good unless it's accessible, and you are physically, mentally, and emotionally prepared to use it. Keep in mind that your weapon can be used against you as well. For this and other reasons, I strongly recommend against women relying on lethal weapons to protect themselves from rape. Nonlethal weapons are safer to use, but they can also fail.

Here are the relative benefits and risks of both lethal and nonlethal weapons, and some caveats regarding martial arts and other self-defense training courses.

Guns

Thousands of people are killed each year in the United States because they own a gun they don't know how to use, or because it falls into the wrong hands.

Benefits: If you are extensively and/or professionally trained in firearm use, and you have a fair amount of experience with your weapon, you may be in a powerful position to protect yourself and others with it. If you are not extensively and/or professionally trained in gun use, a gun's benefits are dramatically outweighed by its risks. For most members of the general public, guns are not a good solution.

Risks: In addition to the always-present risk that your gun will be used against you, you must take on the responsibility and liability of gun ownership.

Before you buy a gun:

You must take an approved safety course with a certified instructor.

You must commit to regular practice with the gun on a firing range.

You must commit to keeping any firearm clean and in good working order.

You should have a trigger lock on it at all times, especially if you have any possibility of children around you or your house.

You must have a secure place to lock up your gun.

You must understand that no gun is any good to you if it is not accessible. In other words, it must be within reach when you are at home, in your car, on a date, or walking on the street. This may be impractical, if not illegal, because most states have laws prohibiting concealed weapons.

You will have to get a permit to carry a gun. You will not be allowed to carry it on public transportation, such as planes, trains, subways, and buses. You cannot carry it while attending sporting events, political meetings, or while in bars. There are many other restrictions pertaining to guns. Check your local laws before you make that purchase.

You must be physically, mentally, and emotionally prepared to instantly use a gun on another human being and take his life, and you must be prepared to accept the legal consequences of that action.

Guns kill, and there is no going back once you have fired one. You must understand that hesitation also kills. The more you think, the longer you will tend to hesitate. The criminal will probably not hesitate in using his weapon. Can you do the same?

The right kind of gun should be appropriate for your size and personality. In most cases, it is ridiculous for a small woman to have a .357 magnum for protection.

Knives

Second only to guns, knives are the most threatening and uncomfortable of all weapons. They are contact weapons, and their effectiveness depends on the ability of the user to handle the weapon and not have it taken away. Because knives are contact weapons, you should understand that if you are close enough to use the knife on the attacker, then he is also close enough to take it from you and use it on you. Knives are potentially lethal, depending on where you stab the attacker, but they are rarely lethal on the first thrust. Usually you would have to stab him over and over again to stop him. Knives, like guns, require the person using them to have made the decision to kill another human being in order for the lethal weapon to work.

Benefits: There aren't many. If you're trained in knife fighting and are prepared to get up close to your attacker, you can do significant damage to him.

Risks: Are you prepared to have a bloody knife fight with a potential rapist? Most women aren't. In most cases, you want to stay as far away from your attacker as possible. The mere thought of physically struggling with a rapist is so terrifying to women that it makes the idea of carrying a knife for protection impractical. You also have to make sure that children do not have access to this weapon. There are laws regulating the length of the blade you can have on a knife.

Nonlethal Weapons

I have taught crime prevention courses for a number of years to hundreds of thousands of people. My research indicates that the average person in most circumstances should not carry a gun or knife for protection. I strongly believe that there are devices available today that are effective, safe, and nonlethal. The greatest benefit of nonlethal weapons is that people will tend to use them without hesitation because they know that even if they make a mistake, no one dies. Still, not all of them are recommended.

Mace (CS or CN Tear Gas)

This nonlethal chemical was developed after World War II. Today, Mace comes in various sizes and shapes. Mace works by chemically stripping away the top layer of oil on the skin. This is done with acetone or some other strong astringent. When the oil is dissolved, the skin's nerve endings are exposed to the CS or CN chemical. This causes a painful, burning sensation, especially in the eyes. The effects last twenty to thirty minutes depending on the individual being sprayed, strength of the chemical, and contact area. If you are attacked, spray the assailant in the face until the container is empty, then immediately escape. Following your escape, you must report the incident to the police.

Benefits: The product is inexpensive and does not require a training process to be able to use it. You just aim at the face and spray. If your attacker is a normal person with an average threshold for pain, Mace will do the trick. It will interrupt the assault long enough for you to escape. Mace is priced from $6 to $50 depending on size and has a range of three to twenty-five feet, depending on the unit and spray pattern. Shelf life is up to two years.

Risks: The attacker will, in many cases, not be stopped if he is under the influence of alcohol or drugs. These substances can raise the threshold for pain to such an extent that the attacker cannot feel the chemical. You also may have a problem if the rapist has thick and/or oily skin. Then the CS/CN tear gas may not be effective, because the thickness and level of oil in the skin may block the chemical. This chemical will not work at all on animals, because the fur and oil on the skin is so thick that the chemical never penetrates. Remember that this kind of non-lethal weapon works best in nonrainy, nonwindy conditions, or when you are upwind from the assailant. This product should be replaced immediately upon its first use because there is no way to measure how much you've used and how much is left in the canister.

Pepper Spray (Oleoresin Capsicum)

This chemical's properties are different from Mace, or CS and CN tear gas. Pepper spray was developed basically to be effective on all those people on whom Mace wouldn't work. Once the Capsicum (derived from the South American Chile Pepper plant) is inhaled into the assailant's nostrils, it restricts the breathing tubes, causing a choking sensation. The attacker will, in most cases, instinctively grab his throat and stop the attack. The pepper also will get into his eyes, and they will not just burn, but will be slammed shut. The product has a two-year shelf life and, like Mace, comes in various sizes and shapes. The chemical's strength is measured in Scoville Heat Units. The more heat it produces, the greater its effectiveness.

Recently, new OC sprays have been developed that are even stronger. You can now get a Pepper Spray with up to 5.3 million Scoville Heat Units. What does that mean? It means that if you had one cup of pepper that was rated at 5.3 million Scoville Heat Units, you would need 5.3 million cups of sugar water to neutralize this heat.

One of the biggest misconceptions about defense sprays is that the higher the percentage of pepper in the spray, the hotter and better it works. In most cases this could not be further from the truth. Most of the best, fastest incapacitating sprays in the world have a content of 2–10 percent pepper. The lighter the fluid, the faster it penetrates the membranes. The percentage has nothing to do with the actual SHU or "heat" in the spray. Also, thicker sprays can inflame the skin area more and last longer with this unnecessary inflammation. A good spray will put most attackers down, which gives you the time and the distance to escape or take control of the situation.

Because it is an inflammatory rather than an irritant, OC is effective against most of those who feel no pain, such as psychotics, drunks, and drug abusers. OC has proven itself to be one of the best deterrents available for attacking dogs and wild animal control. Another major advantage of OC is that it is not volatile, and it will not emit a lot of fumes as tear gases do.

Today the value is established through high technology, a computerized method called high-performance liquid chromatography. The pepper scale ranges from zero Scoville units for a bell pepper to 5,000 or so for a jalapeño to a whopping 200,000–300,000 for a habañero! Pure capsaicin is 15,000,000. The oleoresin capsicum used in a superior pepper spray formula is derived from the hottest peppers and further processed and refined until the heat rating is 5,300,000 (5.3 million!).

I recommend at least two million Scoville Heat Units. Remember, this kind of nonlethal weapon works best in nonrainy, nonwindy conditions, or when you are upwind from the assailant. Once again, after you spray the attacker, escape and report the crime to the police. The pricing is similar to CS and CN tear gas, at $10 to $50.

Benefits: In addition to stopping most assailants who are intoxicated or on drugs, pepper spray can also stop attackers who have a high threshold of pain. This is true because the spray works on the nostrils and lungs. It is also effective on animals. The National Park Service and many animal control personnel have been using pepper spray for a number of years to control dogs, bears, and other animals. This chemical will work on almost all assailants, regardless of skin type, pigmentation, or level of oil on the skin. Its range is three to twenty-five feet, depending on the unit and spray pattern.

Reality Check:
Remember, there are no guarantees with any product or plan of action.

Risks: Pepper spray can and does work most of the time on most individuals, but it does not work on everyone or on every animal. There are cases where an assailant has been sprayed with a pepper spray unit by several police officers, but with no effects.

All chemical sprays are subject to bad manufacturing and leakage. The worst time to find out that your unit is not working is during an assault. You should always test the unit prior to using it in a criminal confrontation. You can't practice with small key-chain sprayers because you will use them up in the process . If you decide to carry Mace or pepper spray, you should carry a larger unit so that you can practice with it, and so that you can have more than one shot at the assailant. You also should be aware that with any chemical device, there is a chance that if you use it against your attacker during an assault, you will get sprayed as well. It's a good idea to prepare yourself for this possibility.

If you get sprayed, do not use any creams or salves, and don't rub your eyes. Most chemicals can be washed off with water. In approximately thirty to forty-five minutes the pain should dissipate, and you should recover. It is wise to consult a doctor if you have an adverse reaction to the chemical.

Like guns, chemical sprays cannot be taken aboard airplanes or onto some other modes of transportation. In many states you cannot carry such devices into an elementary or high school. You cannot carry them into courthouses, government buildings, or other federal facilities. You should check with your local law enforcement agency to see what restrictions govern the carrying and use of chemical sprays.

A Word about Reporting the Crime: Why should you report the crime? If you don't, and if the assailant reports that you've used a weapon on him, you may find yourself arrested for assault. Most law enforcement officials generally assume that, in the case of an altercation, the first person to report the incident is the victim. If you report the incident, you can explain the situation and why you responded as you did, even if it turns out that you overreacted or sprayed an innocent person in error.

Stun Guns

Stun guns are not guns at all but electrical devices similar to cattle prods. They work by shocking the assailant with a bolt of electricity. Their effectiveness depends on many things such as voltage, climate, assailant's clothing, what part of the assailant's body you contact with the stun gun, and the charge of the battery. The part of electricity that stuns is the voltage; the part that kills is the amperage. Stun guns may have 50,000 to 150,000 volts, but they put out electricity at very low amperage. They work by generating electrical charges that make the muscles constrict and expand rapidly. If the contact is in the right place on the body, the assailant's knees will buckle, and he will fall down. This is a fairly expensive nonlethal weapon, ranging in price up to $150. Laws regarding stun guns are a little less restrictive than those for chemical devices because they are contact devices, and they do not run the risk of contaminating a controlled environment's air system.

Benefits: There are few. Stun guns are best as prevention tools. In other words, you can push the button and see a spark fly from one contact point to another and hear an electrical buzzing sound. At night this display of electricity may ward off an attacker.

Risks: There are many. First of all, you must not only make contact with the assailant's side or upper leg, but you must maintain contact for up to seven seconds. This can be an eternity in a criminal confrontation. Remember, if you're close enough to touch him, he is close enough to touch you. This product may or may not work if the attacker is wearing heavy clothes, such as a leather jacket, etc. Stun guns are battery-powered, using nine-volt batteries. A stun gun's battery must be fully charged for the device to work adequately.

Tasers

The Taser is an energy weapon utilizing EMD (electro-muscular disruption) technology. EMD weapons utilize more advanced technology than do traditional stun weapons that operate at a higher voltage but a lower wattage.

Whereas a stun gun or stun baton may operate in ranges from 80,000 to 775,000 volts, a Taser generates between 7 and 14 watts. The applied power interferes with the communication signals of the nervous system, causing temporary loss of coordinated muscular control.

Naturally, the higher voltage stun guns will have a greater effect than lesser voltage units, but their smaller size aids in maintaining the element of surprise. Stun batons are best used for home defense, where concealment is less a concern, and the intimidating size can intensify the "fear factor." Though stun guns can be highly effective in the right circumstances, there is a small percentage of people with a very high pain tolerance who can maintain some limited aggressive capabilities.

The 50,000 volt Taser, with its more powerful 18- to 26-watt pulse, disrupts the central nervous system and directly controls the skeletal muscles causing an uncontrollable contraction of the muscle tissue. The EMD effect overrides voluntary muscle control, even among pain-tolerant, aggressive combatants. The subject will be immobilized quickly and will fall on the ground.

The Taser is aimed at the subject. When the intended victim fires it, two probes attached to 15 feet of trailing wire, are propelled by compressed nitrogen gas at 135 fps (feet per second) The electrical impulse passes to the subject's body where the probes have attached to the body or clothing.

An automatic initial 7-second charge usually disables the attacker, and continual pulses separated by 1.8 second intervals keep the subject from regaining equilibrium or removing the wires. The initial sequence lasts for about thirty seconds. While the subject is dazed and temporarily disabled, the intended victim can escape the threat.

The Taser does not depend on body penetration or impact to work. The powerful pulsating electrical current will jump up to two inches, as long as both probes are attached to skin or clothing. This debilitating jolt is effective, yet it normally causes no damage to nerves, muscles, or other body tissue.

Extensive testing has proven the effectiveness and safety of the Taser. A January 1987 *Annals of Emergency Medicine* study reported no long-term injuries, compared with 50 percent long-term injuries for surviving gun shot victims.

Will the Taser cause electrocution or heart problems?

This stun weapon will not, in most cases, cause electrocution or interfere with a cardiac pacemaker. Medical testing has confirmed that the T-wave will not interrupt the heartbeat or damage a pacemaker. Cardiac defibrillators used to revive heart patients use a current hundreds of times stronger than the T-wave without causing damage. Should your attacker somehow get close enough to touch you, the current will not pass through to you. You will not receive a shock even if you are standing in water at the time.

The ideal range to fire is seven to ten feet away from your attacker. This insures optimum effect. The unit also has a backup touch stun mode should you miss the target or face multiple attackers.

The Taser works well in all seasons. Neither the cold of winter nor the heat of summer affects the compressed nitrogen propellant cartridges or the T-wave.

Civilian use of the Taser is recommended as a surprise defense, though the unit can be quite intimidating. This is especially true of the laser-sight model, as the attacker has little doubt as to if and where he will be hit. Knowing he will absolutely get hit will often convince the attacker to look for easier prey.

In summary, the Taser is a safe, yet highly effective self-defense weapon, especially when compared to more deadly alternatives.

Tasers may be illegal in your area. Check with law enforcement and/or campus security before you buy one. The price range is approximately $50 to $150.

Benefits: Although the Taser is a contact device, the contact is generally not close enough for the attacker to make contact with you. If he is four to six feet from you, you may be able to get away.

Risks: There are many. You only have one shot,, so you'd better make that one shot count. Like stun guns, Tasers are vulnerable because they depend on a fully charged battery. However, the biggest problem is that they are still illegal in many areas.

Household Objects as Weapons

What follows is a partial list of the most common things around the house that people think of as potentially effective weapons against a rapist.

rat tail comb	hair spray	pens/pencils	oven cleaner
umbrella	rolling pin	hat pin	car keys
frying pan	purse/books	tire iron	fireplace tongs

Your goal is to incapacitate your attacker—you must put him on the ground long enough for you to escape. How long is long enough? About twenty to thirty minutes. This gives you enough time to clear the area. If he's on the ground for that amount of time, you have the time to get help or to get to a safe area. Most of the common household items that you may have in your possession or close to you will not incapacitate the criminal; all they will do is hurt him. If you hurt him but don't hurt him enough to stop him, he will definitely hurt you!

. . . .

Reality Check:
In all cases, your only goal is to incapacitate him
long enough for you to escape.

. . . .

Weapons Can Fail

As with any man-made device, a weapon is subject to malfunctions and user error. There is no weapon that always works on everyone in all conditions. You take your chances with any lethal or nonlethal weapon. Don't think that just because you have a weapon, you can let your guard down. Your best weapon is your mind. Use it and trust your inner guidance to tell you what to do. There are no guarantees: whether you carry a weapon or not, whether you take a self-defense course or not, you still can be assaulted.

Martial Arts and Self-Defense Courses

Before you invest in a self-defense course, understand that there is a great difference between the fantasy of the martial arts movies and the reality of street combat. Assailants don't fight fair, and they will not pull their punches or abide by classroom rules. In a confrontation, everything happens very quickly. You should not realistically expect to become proficient in any martial arts discipline in a few short hours or weeks. Achieving proficiency will take time and intensive commitment. What you may decide to do, as do many women, is to take a self-defense course, which can empower you with a few techniques and ideas to interrupt an assault long enough to escape.

Why Self-Defense Courses?

What is the difference between martial arts courses and self-defense courses?

There is a large distinction between the majority of martial arts and pure self-defense. Most martial arts offer long-term programs, often with many levels (belts) to be achieved, requiring the memorization of a series of choreographed techniques, one-step techniques, controlled sparring, the study of various weapons, etc.

Most women seek information on how to stay safe and/or fight back, and they are not interested in spending four to six years studying a martial art in order to feel more secure. Self-defense is a conscious, proactive, methodical approach to life. It comprises a series of both learned and intrinsic behavioral and cognitive options that you must choose to put to work for you. And it may include a series of physical self-defense options that could be used, as a last resort, if you were to be physically attacked.

What can I learn?

A good self-defense course can provide many benefits. The following are some important areas that should be covered:

- Facts and figures about crime and self-defense.
- Myths that keep violence against women in place and growing.
- Cognitive and behavioral options—tools such as awareness and intuition that can be used to avoid violent crime.
- Boundary-setting information—how to communicate "no!"
- Physical self-defense techniques that an average person can easily learn, practice, and use if necessary. Courses that use padded male attackers, when presented safely and consciously, offer the most real-life training experience.
- Information resources—survivor information and safety tips.

Where do I start?

If you're looking for a good self-defense course in your area, and you're not sure where to start, here are some ideas on where to turn: friends and relatives, rape crisis centers, private therapists and counselors, local colleges and universities, local Ys, fitness centers, your state network against sexual assault, local law enforcement agencies, local martial arts schools (some martial arts schools offer self-defense seminars separately from the regular curriculum.)

What questions should I ask?

- Who is the instructor? Is the instructor male or female?
- What does the course teach? Does it offer a well-rounded curriculum with both physical and behavioral options?
- Will I have to "relive" or "recreate" an attack if I have experienced one in the past? (If you have survived a sexual or other assault, you

may not want to relive it in front of a class. Select a teacher who does not require you to do that if you don't want to. However, learning how to fight and being able to practice on a padded attacker is enormously empowering for a lot of people.)
- Is the course appropriate for my age group and level of previous experience or skill?
- Where, when, how much, and how long is the course?

(This information comes from The National Coalition Against Sexual Assault website's guidelines for selecting a self-defense course.)

As with any choice in life, there is much to be said for listening to your intuitive feelings. If it feels right to you, go with it. But do a little homework before you decide on a course. Make sure it's the right time, mentally and emotionally, for you to take this step.

Remember, there are no guarantees. You can still be victimized even if you have taken a self-defense course or mastered a martial arts discipline. Once you've completed a self-defense course or become practiced in martial arts training, it's up to you to put the information you gained to work for you in your day-to-day life.

Realize that if you are attacked after having completed one of these courses, your ability to effectively use the physical self-defense options that you learned will be dependent upon your ability to remember what you learned in the course and your willingness to practice—with intensity and regularity—those techniques.

Use creative visualization—imagine getting attacked in a variety of environments and then see yourself using what you learned to defeat your attacker and emerge successfully from the situation. For more detailed information, see the National Coalition Against Sexual Assault website at www.ncasa.org/.

Surviving and Recovering from Sexual Assault

Chapter Eleven

After the Assault

If you have been raped or have experienced an attempted rape, you are not alone and you do not need to suffer alone.

Your immediate goal after the assault is to get to safety as quickly as possible. Your long-term goals are to recover physically, mentally, and emotionally, and to take back control of your body and your life so you can forge a stronger identity as a result of what has happened.

Whether you decided to fight with all of your strength, put up some resistance, or not fight back at all, you did not ask or deserve to be violated. Even if the rapist was not successful in completing his assault on you, you have been violated. You may tend to judge yourself for your actions or lack of actions during the assault, but no one, no matter what she has done, deserves to be raped. After the assault, be gentle on yourself. It was not your fault, no matter what you did or did not do.

> **Sexual assault victims would be more likely to report the crime if they did not fear becoming entangled in the morass of an insensitive criminal justice system.**
>
> —Assistant Attorney General Lois H. Herrington, 1985

Ten Things You Must (or Must Not) Do if You Have Been Raped

1. Get away from the rapist and get to safety.
2. Do not shower, bathe, douche, wash your hands, brush your teeth, or use the toilet. (If you do, you will destroy evidence of the assault.)
3. Do not change your clothing. (Again, this may destroy evidence.)
4. Do not straighten up your house or apartment if it was the scene of the crime. (Difficult as it may be not to, you may destroy important evidence if you do.)
5. Report the crime. (Call the police and campus security.)
6. Get a medical evidentiary exam. (Call your doctor, your health service, the local hospital, or a crisis center to find out where to go.)
7. Call someone whom you trust to be with you. (This person can make phone calls for you and accompany you to the police station or hospital. You may wish to have this person stay overnight with you.)
8. Contact a rape crisis center. (They will provide you with a great deal of information, as well as understanding and support.)
9. Get into counseling. (Find a good therapist, support group, etc.)
10. Be gentle on yourself. (Rape is a violent, life-threatening crime. Recovery takes time.)

Reasons to Report the Assault

Many women do not seek help for various reasons. Among them are their fears that the system will not be sensitive to their needs. They may not be aware of the resources in their area or they may want to minimize the severity of the crime. In date rape situations, there may be additional reasons that have to do with the relationship of the victim to the rapist, the status or connections of the rapist, or else the criminal is so popular or well known that the victim feels no one would believe her. Knowing what to expect when you report the crime can diffuse your fears of the unknown.

There are countless reasons why you should report the assault:

- Police can help you get to a safe place and get a medical examination.
- Reporting the crime can help the police keep the rapist from attacking other women in the future.
- It is your right and responsibility. The only reason there are so many rape crisis centers and public support groups for victims is because women like yourself had the courage to come forward and report an assault regardless of the circumstances and/or consequences.
- Colleges are more likely to take actions to stop date rape if they are convinced there is a problem. Reporting the rape makes them aware.
- Reporting the assault will get you in touch with rape crisis and counseling centers, which you need to contact as soon as possible after the crime in order to recover as fully and rapidly as possible.
- You may be entitled to compensation. Many states have instituted victim compensation laws in which crime victims can apply for monetary awards from the state to pay for medical exams and physical therapy.
- Reporting the crime immediately after it occurs will help your credibility. However, even if you do not file a report, it does not mean the crime did not occur.
- Some rapists attack their victims again and will not stop their assaults until the police get involved. Sometimes, a rapist will end the assault with a threat that if you report the crime, he will come back and hurt you. Even if you comply, he may still harm you, and your compliance may cause him to think he can victimize you and get away with it. Reporting the assault, however, sends him a message that he cannot intimidate you and puts you back in control. Police intervention may be your best protection.
- Reporting the crime does not necessarily mean that you have to prosecute the attacker, but if you report it, you keep your options open in case you decide to prosecute at a later date.
- Keeping silent can hurt you psychologically and emotionally, and may inhibit your ability to get beyond the trauma.
- Rape crisis counselors, friends, family, etc., cannot help you unless they know about the incident. There are people out there who have been in your place and can help you get beyond this. You are not alone.

Reality Check:
You have a choice to make—to do what is best for
the rapist or to do what is best for you!

Following are some of the things you can expect when you report the rape to the police. These procedures are taken from *Recovering from Rape* by Linda E. Ledray, R.N., Ph.D., and from Surviving Sexual Assault by the Los Angeles Commission on Assaults Against Women. The individual procedures in your area may differ. The crime must be reported in the jurisdiction where the assault occurred. You may not be aware that many communities have psychologically trained investigative units that specialize in rape cases. These people have your interests at heart and will be sensitive to your feelings. (Please note that these units are more likely to be found in large metropolitan areas.)

The Medical and Evidentiary Exams

The following information will tell you not only what will happen during the medical examination process but also what your rights are. Even if you were able to escape before being raped, it is advisable for you to seek medical attention. There are four reasons why you need to get a medical exam immediately after the assault:

1. To calculate the extent of your injuries. It is common for the victim of a rape or attempted rape to go into a state of shock and numbness in which she will not realize the extent of her injuries.
2. To collect medical evidence for possible future prosecution. This evidence must be gathered as soon as possible. If you can be tested within twelve hours of the rape, there is a 95 percent chance the test for sperm and semen will be accurate.[14] The longer you wait, the more difficult it will be for the doctors to obtain usable specimens.
3. To settle fears you may have about AIDS or venereal disease.
4. To be tested for preexisting pregnancy.

It is a good idea for you to call a supportive friend to come with you or meet you at the hospital. Have your friend bring an extra set of clothes for you as your present clothes may be taken from you to be used as evidence of the assault. You may want to have a female friend meet you, as she may be more supportive than a boyfriend or family member right now.

Where do you go to get the examination? If you decide to report the rape to the police, they will know which hospitals have the services that you need. They also can put you in touch with a rape crisis center for counseling. If you decide not to report it, you can call your doctor for advice as to where to go.

Once you know which hospital to use, you should go to the emergency room, where, unfortunately, you may not be a high priority, especially if you have no outward signs of physical injury. This may mean that you will have to wait until the emergency staff is available to help you. The emergency room may not be warm, comfortable, or at all pleasant for you, especially at this time. In fact, it will probably be bright, cold, and impersonal. Be prepared for this—don't let it keep you from seeking medical attention. Any hospital that deals with sexual assaults should have a sensitively trained team of doctors, nurses, and psychologists who will help you through the process. Just in case you encounter impersonal or insensitive hospital staff, it is important to have a supportive friend accompany and help you during this exam.

During a medical exam:
- You may wish to call your personal physician to be with you during this procedure.
- Insist on being treated with gentleness and sensitivity.
- You can request privacy during the collection of medical evidence. If you are a minor, your right to have the exam take place without parents or guardians present will depend on local laws.
- You may request that police officers leave the examination room during the actual exam.
- You may request that a friend, family member, or rape crisis counselor be present during the exam.

- You have the right to have each procedure explained in detail before you allow the doctors to continue with the exam. Make sure you understand what the doctors and nurses are telling you. If you cannot decipher the medical terminology, ask them to stop and explain it to you.
- The evidentiary exam is an examination for the purpose of obtaining evidence of sexual assault. It may include a pelvic exam. If forced sodomy or forced oral sex was performed, additional exams may be required of other parts of your body.

The evidentiary exam will document evidence of recent sexual intercourse, signs of force, and anything that could identify and incriminate the assailant.

Evidence of Recent Sexual Intercourse
The proof of recent sexual intercourse will be obtained by a collection of seminal fluids, sperm, vaginal secretions, secretions from any other bodily areas involved in the rape, and samples of pubic hair. The absence of sperm does not mean that intercourse did not occur—many rapists are sexually dysfunctional, at least during the rape, and do not ejaculate during the assault.

Evidence of Force
It is important that evidence be obtained to establish proof that the sexual intercourse was forced or against your will. The following steps may be taken:

Photographs may be taken of any bruises, abrasions, or injuries. Because bruises often do not appear for twenty-four to forty-eight hours, you may wish to request that the police take a second set of pictures at a later date when they become visible. (These pictures are useless as evidence if you take them yourself.)

Torn or soiled clothing worn during the rape will be held by the police for evidence. If you want it back, you will need to ask for it. Lack of physical signs of force does not mean that force was not used. Date rapists often use minimal physical force but will use extreme emotional and mental intimidation, which can have the same paralyzing effect on the victim as actual violence.

Blood samples may be taken to ascertain whether drugs and/or alcohol are in your system. This is likely if you indicate that you've used drugs or if you believe you have been drugged by the assailant. This evidence can show that you were not in control of your faculties at the time of the rape.

Exam Questions

The doctors and/or medical personnel may require a urine sample for pregnancy testing and may ask the following questions prior to the evidentiary exam:

What is your medical history?

What is your marital status?

What was the date of your last period?

Is your menstrual cycle regular?

Are you currently using birth control?

Have you ever been pregnant? If so, did you have a live birth, miscarriage, or abortion?

What was the date of your last sexual intercourse prior to the assault?

What is your recent sexual history?

Was the attacker using a condom?

You may find some of these questions personal and private, but understand that procedures and testing depend upon your answers.

Incriminating Evidence

This physical evidence is needed to build a case against the rapist. It may start to disintegrate with the passage of time. Some of the physical evidence also may disintegrate because of the weather. If you were raped outside, there may be physical signs of the attack that will be destroyed if it rains. This is another reason to report the assault as soon as possible.

A collection of the following may be taken to help build the State's case against the assailant: seminal fluids to determine the rapist's blood type;

foreign matter still on your body such as leaves, fibers, hairs, etc., that will be used to identify your attacker.

After the evidentiary exam, you may wish to request copies of all medical reports. The victim assistance program in your area may be able to reimburse you for the expenses of your exams. You may request help in filling out the necessary forms to qualify for financial assistance. You have the right to strict medical confidentiality.

Pregnancy Testing

A urine specimen will be taken to determine if you were pregnant before the rape. You should be tested again to determine if you have become pregnant as a result of the rape. Some states will pay for this follow-up exam as part of the evidentiary exam if you have reported the rape within thirty-six hours of the assault.

If you do become pregnant, continue to seek advice from the rape crisis center and other qualified professionals who will continue to support you after you make a decision about your pregnancy. Your rape crisis counselor can do much to help you get into support groups whatever your decision may be.

Dealing with the Police and the Courts

Rape and attempted rape are both crimes, and as such will involve the police and the court system. The following information is not meant to overwhelm you with the legal process or scare you into not reporting the crime or prosecuting the rapist, but to let you know what will happen so that you can be prepared to handle it.

The Police

Call the general police phone number in your local telephone directory to verify jurisdiction of the precinct where the crime occurred. If you are unable to call, have someone call for you. It may be easier for you if you have a supportive friend with you. Your first inclination may be to call your boyfriend, lover, brother, or parents to go to the police station with you. If they are totally supportive and can handle it, they can be enormously helpful to you. However, many victims of rape find their families' embarrassment, fear, anger, and guilt may cause them to behave in unexpected ways. Choose a friend, a rape crisis counselor, or someone who will not judge you.

The police will probably ask you to come to the police station to file a report. If you are unable for physical or emotional reasons to go to the station, they may send officers to you wherever you are.

In filing a crime report with the police, you will be asked:

- Your name, address, place of employment, phone number, date, time, and location of the assault; and a description of the assailant.
- The details of the assault. This may be difficult for you, but they need to know. What happened? What did he do to you? What did he say to you? Try to be as accurate as possible and try to recall his exact words. Something he said may seem insignificant, but the police may be able to connect him to other assaults through his words or actions. The accuracy of your statements also will help your case during prosecution.
- Your activities before and after the attack. This may seem unnecessary, but again something about your activities before or after might become a clue as to why you were singled out.
- If you were drinking or using drugs. It is better to include this information in your report now. The detectives are not there to arrest you for your conduct—they are investigating a rape. Besides, if you do not include it now and decide to prosecute later, the rapist's defense attorney may discover it and use this information to discredit your testimony.

You may be in such a state of shock that it is difficult for you to tell your story. If you would feel more comfortable dealing with a female officer, ask for one. If you were raped or assaulted by a stranger, you may be asked to look at mug shots and assist in making a composite picture. Do not be too hard on yourself if you cannot remember what he looks like. You have just come through a life-threatening situation. You may be in shock. Be patient, as your memory may come back to you later.

You might also be asked to identify a suspect in a lineup. This is generally done through a one-way glass or a specially lit room so that the suspect cannot see you.

After you make your report, you have the right to police transportation to your home. (If the assault occurred at your home or apartment, you may wish to be taken to another place.)

....

Reality Check:

The police are not there to judge you. If any of their questions seem improper or accusatory, you have the right to ask: why this information is necessary? You did not commit the assault—the rapist did. If the police seem to forget this fact, remind them that you or your actions are not on trial here.

....

If you do not hear from the police in one or two days, you have the right to call and ask to whom the case has been assigned and about the current status of the investigation. Keep in touch with those assigned to your case. If you think of any information that was not included in your report, do not hesitate to call to have it included. Everything is important!

You may also be interviewed by the prosecutor's office and have to tell your story again. The prosecutor will decide whether there is sufficient admissible evidence to issue a formal complaint. Even if the state decides not to prosecute, that does not mean that the assault did not happen. It may only mean that there is insufficient evidence to gain a conviction.

The Criminal Courts

If the state does decide to prosecute, the suspect will be arraigned before a judge. You may or may not be required to attend.

If the suspect pleads not guilty, a hearing is set, and you may be sub-poenaed to testify at this hearing. It should take place within ten days (customarily within seventy-two hours) after the suspect is arrested, but delays are common.

If the judge presiding at the arraignment decides there is enough evidence, the case will go to trial. The suspect may be arraigned in court or, if he pleads guilty, the suspect will be charged and sentenced. You may not have to attend the pretrial hearing.

Your presence is required at the actual trial. The prosecuting attorney does not represent you; he or she represents the state because the defendant has broken the laws of the state. The prosecution is hired by the state, not by you. However, you are the star witness for the prosecution.

If convicted, the rapist is sentenced. If he is acquitted (due to lack of evidence), it does not mean you were not raped. It means only that the state could not prove its case beyond a reasonable doubt.

A trial can be a long and drawn-out process. You will need all the support you can get before, during, and after the trial. Get in touch with the rape crisis center and the victim assistance program in your area. They can help you understand what is happening in court and they may be able to help you with transportation to and from court if you need it. Get counseling or get into a survivors' support group. The local rape crisis center can give you information on the groups in your area.

The Civil Courts

You may wish to sue the rapist for damages. This is a civil suit, and it requires the services of an attorney, for which you will have to pay. This attorney, unlike the District Attorney, represents you and not the state.

Even if the assailant has no funds to pay you after a judgment is obtained against him, he is identified and embarrassed as a rapist. State laws may differ, but a judgment against him may interfere with his ability to buy or own certain property until the judgment is satisfied.

It is important to understand that the requirements (evidence and degree of proof) are not the same in a civil suit as they are in a criminal proceeding. Even if you lose the criminal case against your attacker, you may win monetary damages from him in a civil court. Note that in a civil proceeding you may be required to testify as to your sexual history. This generally will not be asked of you in a criminal proceeding.

Chapter Twelve

Physical and Emotional Recovery

Whether you decided to fight or not, giving in to a rapist is not shameful. Rape is a violent crime. It is life threatening. If you survived, you did the right thing, no matter what anyone else says. Getting on with your life is your utmost concern. Remember, you can heal only if you are alive!

Rape and sexual assault are traumas that may interrupt your life at home, work, or school, affecting your relationships with friends, family, and coworker.

Although the process of recovery is often slow and confusing, with understanding and persistence you can accomplish a great deal. You have control over how you recover. The reassurance and support of friends, family, or your significant other is very important during this time, but their reaction to your experience may not be what you anticipate or would like it to be. People in your life will react in different ways—some may express blame, others may give you their full support. If you feel ready, you should allow those who offer their support to help you through this period—it will aid you in your recovery process. The decision to talk about your experience is a personal choice. You do not have to share your experience with anyone until you feel ready.

What You Deserve as a Survivor

You have survived an attack on your life. During the possibly chaotic aftermath of your experience, you may find yourself having to stick up for yourself and be your own advocate. Even though it is likely that your self-esteem has suffered as a result of your experience, keep in mind that you deserve nothing less than supportive, loving, caring treatment from everyone you encounter. Anyone who does not treat you well should be reminded of this. You deserve

- To be believed
- To be given the same credibility as any other crime victim
- To seek help
- Courteous, efficient treatment
- To be treated with dignity and respect, without prejudice against race, class, lifestyle, age, sex, or occupation
- Accurate information, presented in a way that you understand
- To have your questions answered
- To make your own decisions
- To get help and support from others
- To heal fully and completely and to take all the time you need to do so

Your Individual Response

Your response to the assault can cover a wide range of physical and emotional symptoms, even some that may not seem to result directly from the attack. When you learn to recognize these symptoms, it will help you to gain control of them. Not every victim experiences all of these responses, and the following list only suggests several possibilities. You may experience these symptoms immediately, or after months—maybe even years later—or you may never experience any of them. It all depends on each individual and the support you get from the people around you.

Common Emotional Reactions to Sexual Assault

Emotional Shock: Feeling numb, can't cry.
Disbelief: Questioning the event—Why me?
Embarrassment: What will people think?

Shame: Feeling dirty.

Guilt: It is my fault. If only I had . . . , etc.

Depression: Feeling tired and hopeless.

Powerlessness: Feeling out of control.

Disorientation: Feeling overwhelmed; can't sit still.

Retriggering: Having flashbacks of the assault.

Denial: Minimizing the impact of the experience.

Fear: Having nightmares; fearing pregnancy, AIDS, sexually transmitted diseases, intimacy; fearing that you are going crazy.

Anxiety: Having trouble breathing; experiencing muscle tension; having difficulty sleeping; experiencing loss of appetite, nausea, stomach problems, nightmares, or bed-wetting.

Anger: Wanting to get even. Wanting to kill the attacker.

Emotional Response

Rape survivors react in different ways after they have been raped, depending on many factors. There is no normal or abnormal, good or bad, right or wrong response to being sexually assaulted. A woman's reactions may depend upon her sense of self-worth before the assault, the extent of her relationship with the attacker, and the resources available to her after the attack. Her family dynamics (whether she will be blamed or shunned for being raped) and the amount of sincere support and caring her friends show after the rape also will affect the healing process greatly.

In the book *Recovering from Rape*, Linda E. Ledray, R.N., Ph.D., indicates some of the stages a rape survivor might face. The following reactions may occur in any order and be experienced at different intervals. You may stay in one stage for a long time, or you may skip one or more stages entirely. If you feel stuck in a particular stage for a long time, your counselor, therapist, or support group may be able to help you.

Emotional Shock and Disbelief—"Why Me?"

You may believe that rape cannot happen to good girls or that a rapist cannot possibly be a guy you know. If you believe the male-created myths that women who are raped wanted, provoked, or deserved the attack, you may be in shock, and it may be more difficult for you to believe that the rape actually happened to you. You may feel numb and unable to cry. You may block out the rape and find it difficult to remember anything but the time before or after the rape. As you begin to get stronger and emotionally more able to deal with the assault, flashbacks and nightmares may occur. You also may feel weak, have trouble sleeping, and feel exhausted.

Embarrassment, Shame, Guilt

"I'm ashamed to tell anyone." "I can't tell my parents; they'd think I made it up." These are some of the things women say when they are feeling shame, guilt, or embarrassment about a date rape situation. Feeling embarrassed about being raped is a form of taking responsibility for the man's behavior. Not only have women suffered from rape and other forms of sexual assault, but they have also been ostracized by family and community for being victims. Your husband, boyfriend, family, or friends may not understand. Find someone who does. There is nothing for you to be ashamed of. You are not the rapist. He is the one who should be ashamed! Stand up for yourself and refuse to let anyone blame you for being victimized.

Disorientation

You may feel disoriented and confused by all that has happened to you as well as being inundated by the demands being put upon you at this time. There are important decisions that have to be made, and even though you are in no emotional condition to think rationally, you still have to make them. This is another reason to contact a rape crisis counselor and/or support group who can empathize with what you are going through. You are not alone.

Anger, Rage, Revenge Fantasies

It is perfectly acceptable and normal to be angry with your attacker. In fact, it can be very healthy to be angry, because anger can become a motivating force out of the feelings of helplessness, powerlessness, and worthlessness. Often, the feelings of anger and rage do not come until later, which is unfortunate because it can be easier to make decisions about your welfare if you have the energy of anger. You also may have thoughts and fantasies of elaborate revenge. Do not be too concerned about these feelings and fantasies—they are natural.

Depression

During the few days after the assault, you may experience depression. The severity of the feelings after the rape may be confusing to you, especially if you are being told by other people, "You're okay, just forget about it," or, "You're not hurt so what's the big deal?"

On an unconscious level, the impulse of family members and friends— even though they love you and have the best intentions in mind—is to minimize what has happened to you. This is a defense mechanism that enables them to deal with guilt they may be feeling for not having been able to protect you.

A common reaction to surviving a life-threatening situation is to become depressed. Depression may cause you to feel the following:

Discouraged about the future

That you have nothing to live for or that things are hopeless

An exaggerated feeling about your faults, and seeing only the worst side of yourself

Depression can be self-perpetuating and can last for an extended period, especially after the trauma of rape. Depression should not be ignored, as it is treatable and may get worse if not addressed.

Fear

When a woman is raped or sexually assaulted, she may fear the rapist and anyone who resembles him. In a date rape situation, a woman's trust of familiar men can be destroyed, leading to a total lack of trust in any and all men. She may lump all men together as potential rapists. Even boyfriends, lovers, and husbands are not immune to being considered in the same category as the rapist. It may be difficult for her to trust men.

She may distrust her ability to differentiate a good (safe) man from a bad (dangerous) man.

Retriggering

This is when something or someone reminds you of the rape. Often on the one-year anniversary of the assault, the survivor will have an emotional reaction. This can also happen if the rape occurred in a particular place like a parking garage in which case any parking garage could trigger an emotional reaction, because it reminds the woman of where she was raped. In date rape, this can be exacerbated because the rapist is often in contact with the victim after the rape. The trauma may be so great because of continual retriggering incidents that the victim might leave her job or school, or move away, just to stop the memories from recurring.

Other Physical and Emotional Reactions

You may become more dependent on friends and family or you may feel compelled to withdraw from people. It is common to have low self-esteem and to want to change your appearance so as to repel anyone who might be interested in you sexually.

Along with or as a result of the emotional responses, a sexual assault survivor may experience a wide range of physical responses, including muscle tension, pain, shortness of breath, gynecological disturbances, fatigue, and changes in sleeping and eating patterns.

Feelings of despair may be temporary and pass quickly, but, when a life-threatening crisis like rape occurs, everything is serious and nothing should be taken for granted. If thoughts of suicide or self-harm occur, realize that they are normal, but a rape crisis counselor or therapist should be consulted at once.

Sexual dysfunction and promiscuity can occur in the aftermath of rape. Sexual dysfunction usually occurs if the victim views sex as synonymous with rape. If promiscuity occurs after a rape, it can be the most difficult for friends and family to understand, and it often gives them an excuse to disbelieve the woman's story.

Many people have rigid expectations of the way a woman is supposed to behave after she has been raped, expecting her to act hysterical, to sob, and to have shredded clothes and black and blue marks from fighting off the rapist. If her behavior is not consistent with these expectations, others may disbelieve her.

Some of her girlfriends may minimize the assault or appear to blame the victim because they feel threatened—if their friend was an innocent victim, then perhaps they could be too. It may be easier to blame their friend instead of the rapist. Her friends may feel safer if they believe she caused the attack or made it up. Even her friends and family may seem tired of talking about the incident. This is also a way of denying that what happened was important and worth remembering.

Many people—family, friends, pastors, husbands, and others—will often get fed up with a woman's inability to forgive and forget, and to get on with her life. Forgiveness, which is the ultimate healer, cannot be embraced until she has worked through all of her other feelings in connection with the assault. These include anger, rage, hatred, fear, depression, and helplessness. There are no easy answers to recovery from this devastating crime. A rape victim may or may not ever forgive her attacker. Those who place unrealistic or simplistic solutions on her recovery need to educate themselves as to the reality of rape survival.

Post-Traumatic Stress Disorder

If you have experienced a sexual assault, you may be left with painful wounds others can't see but that you know are there. Post-traumatic stress disorder (PTSD) can occur when normal people experience a terrifying situation they cannot control. In cases of sexual assault, PTSD symptoms can intrude into daily life and prevent a victim from working, having a relationship, or completing everyday tasks. If you feel this is happening, you may want to seek help. A counselor can help you identify and overcome PTSD.

Survivors with PTSD might encounter
- Intrusive flashbacks, dreams, a need to dwell on the assault
- Persistent or intense distress, anxiety, panic attacks, stress, sleep disturbance, irritability, fear, anger, apprehension, indecision, difficulty in concentrating, being easily startled, and sensitivity
- Feelings of detachment or alienation
- Persistent avoidance of people, places, and things associated with the assault
- Ambivalence or uncertainties about the future

• Avoidance of normal daily activity
• Depression
• Reliving the event as if it were still occurring

What to Do to Help Yourself

You must take care of yourself physically and emotionally. The idea of seeing a doctor may seem unpleasant, but it is important for you to get medical attention. You don't have to go alone. Having a family member or friend with you during the examination can help you feel at ease during the procedures. Your rape crisis counselor may be able to arrange for an advocate to accompany you.

A survivor of sexual assault may experience any or all of the following:

Feeling dirty	Anxiety
Shock/numbness	Embarrassment
Loss of control over one's life	Relief
Fear	Grief
Sadness/depression	Loss of trust
Anger	Irritability
Suicidal thoughts	Denial
Preoccupation with safety	Guilt or self-blame
Shame	Apprehension
Indecision	Feeling stuck
Changes in perception of the world	

Ask your medical professional to explain what he or she is doing before the examination, so that you know what to expect. Make sure your doctor understands your situation. You may be more sensitive than the average patient and may need more understanding, more time, or more reassurance during medical procedures, no matter how routine.

You can get treatment for your physical injuries and be tested for sexually transmitted diseases (STDs), including HIV, either at the hospital or by your private doctor. Early detection of STDs is very important. Discuss any medical concerns you have with your doctor or counselor, but don't let these concerns prevent you from receiving the medical treatment you need and deserve. Many rape survivors find that receiving medical attention helps them to regain a sense of control over their bodies.

Many rape survivors feel isolated in the aftermath of the assault. In order to reduce those feelings, reach out for support to those who are close to you: call family members, friends, or a rape crisis counselor. It might help you feel better to have someone to talk to, and you might want people around you for safety.

Consider professional support or counseling. Having someone to talk to about how you are feeling may help you to deal with the emotions you are experiencing because of the rape. Additionally, a counselor can help you build your relationships, express your needs to others, and get those needs met.

Give yourself some time off. You need time to recuperate. You may tend to want to forget what happened to you and get back to work or school as if nothing happened. This is denial, and it will eventually inhibit or prolong your emotional healing. Sooner or later, the trauma will surface consciously or unconsciously and keep surfacing until you take the time and energy to deal with it. Just as with a physical injury to the body, you need time to heal. The mind and heart need time to heal as well. Just because you cannot see the emotional injuries doesn't mean they have not occurred and that you're healed.

Start your healing process by realizing that you have choices as to how you react and how you view the assault. Keep repeating that it was not your fault. The tidal wave of feelings that may be happening to you now does not have to incapacitate you, if you realize that in order to get a handle on your feelings you must begin working with the way you think. Thoughts about the attack and the attacker may continue to pop up inside your head from time to time, but recognize that it is up to you to decide as to what extent they will immobilize you.

There are many techniques and resources that will support you in your journey to healing. I have personally witnessed the effectiveness of affirmations, prayer, and other body/mind/spirit approaches. The "Suggested Reading" section of this book (on p. 211) contains some of my recommendations for books, tapes, and videos. Visit a women's bookstore or a health food store to find more resources.

Individual and Group Counseling

Sexual assault can change your feelings about yourself and those around you. You may not feel the way you did before the assault—physically, emotionally, socially, or sexually. Counseling can help you to deal with these issues and aid you in your recovery.

Victim services or rape crisis counselors will listen, clarify, support, and explore options with you. Individual counseling sessions with a supportive counselor can help you identify issues you would like to resolve surrounding the assault. Together, you will develop appropriate, attainable goals for yourself.

Group counseling will give you the opportunity to share your feelings with other victims, and although each person recovers at a different pace, group counseling provides an environment in which survivors can share their experiences along with their techniques for recovery. Many group members find inspiration and motivation listening to the stories of other victims, and get a unique kind of support for returning to the lives they led before the victimization.

Consider Your Legal Rights

One of the most important decisions you may struggle with is whether or not to report the crime to the police. You may report the crime and still decide not to prosecute. By reporting, you may become eligible for crime victim compensation that will pay for medical costs such as counseling.

Speak with a counselor or with someone you trust to help you determine which decision would be the best for you. Whether you decide to press charges or not, you deserve support. The following list may help you feel better about your experiences since the assault:

- Accept that many of your responses are normal, even if they do not feel comfortable. Coping means different things to different people.
- Develop a routine that is comfortable and that has a positive outcome.

Having a routine can be very stabilizing in the face of traumatic stress.
- Recognize that your assault will affect others around you.
- Develop strategies for gaining support and understanding. Different strategies will be effective with different people.
- Take care of your health. A regular diet can lead to well-being. Sugar and caffeine can increase your stress level.
- Alcohol and drugs may delay some reactions and ultimately make them worse. If you find you are abusing alcohol or drugs, you should contact a counselor immediately.
- Allow time for adequate amounts of rest and relaxation. Some techniques to consider are meditation, deep breathing, listening to music, reading, religious rituals, or anything that focuses and relaxes you.
- Physical activity is a great stress reducer, even if it's just a short walk. Try to exercise every day.
- Supportive listeners can include friends, family, religious leaders, teachers, professional counselors, or counseling groups.
- Patience and understanding are important in the recovery process. It takes time. In addition to the support of friends, family, and loved ones, there are also professional counselors who can assist you.

Reality Check:
Rape is a crime of power over another person.
During the rape or attempted rape, the rapist takes your power away from you by force or intimidation.
After the rape, take your power back.

Don't Give Up
Long after the physical body has healed from the assault, the emotional and mental healing will continue. Some experts and psychologists have indicated that the emotional impact of sexual assault can continue for years after the attack. Don't give up five minutes before the miracle. The emotional recovery from an acquaintance rape often takes much longer than if it was a stranger rape situation. This is because there is an

unspoken bond of trust that exists in every dating situation; this is destroyed in a rape or even in an attempted rape. This destruction of trust is very serious and substantially inhibits the normal healing process. When that trust has been violated, it takes longer for a woman to trust men whether she knows them or not. Most women are familiar with the possibility of assault from a stranger, but not from men they know and trust. That is what makes date and acquaintance rape so insidious.

It is important to remember that he made a deliberate choice to take from you privacy, your sense of safety, your trust, and your control of your life and body. It was not your fault. He was perfectly able to stop. He simply chose not to, no matter what you said or did.

It's not your fault!

No matter how stupid you may feel,
No matter if you knew the guy,
No matter if you were high on drugs/alcohol,
No matter if you originally said, "yes," then said, "no,"
No matter if you've had sex with him before,
No matter if no one believes you,
No matter if you choose not to report it,
No matter what happened, it's not your fault!

The emotional roller coaster that happens after a date rape can last for years, but the length of recovery can be reduced if you get professional help for yourself. It is natural to want to deny what has happened and get on with the rest of your life. However, the fears, anger, rage, panic attacks, feelings of worthlessness, and the occasional feeling that you may be going crazy cannot be buried or denied for long. Sooner or later, these feelings will surface, and when they do, they may adversely affect your other relationships, especially with lovers, husbands, friends, or family. Your job and your ability to function also may be affected

Getting help from a qualified rape crisis counselor or therapist will help you deal with the complex and potentially self-destructive feelings that you may be going through. No one who has survived a rape or attempted rape deserves to be judged. What she needs, as do all rape survivors, is support, understanding, and help in her recovery.

....

Reality Check:
Rape is one of the only crimes in which society
tends to blame the victim.

....

Spiritual Healing

In this chapter, I have talked about mental and emotional healing, but there is another aspect of ourselves that I have not talked about. This is spiritual recovery.

Women who have been raped have been shunned by their families, friends, and husbands, and, in some cultures, the prevalent belief is that the victim has "sinned against God" and was therefore being punished. No belief is as destructive to a woman's self-worth as this. If you are religious, you may be torturing yourself with these feelings. You can counteract these negative emotions by repeating the following statements to yourself:

I accept that I have been violated.

I accept that I am starting to cope with my feelings about the assault.

I accept the anger that I feel about my violation, but understand that my anger can be a temporary part of my recovery, and I have control over whether it intrudes into my life in an inappropriate way.

I give myself permission to talk about my experience with a trusted counselor or therapist.

As I understand my feelings about the assault, I realize that I am on the road to recovery.

I can and do give the responsibility for the assault to the perpetrator of the crime.

I did the best that I could in preventing the assault, and I am determined to do the best I can in my recovery.

My self-esteem is increasing as I learn to value myself a little more each day.

I am learning more each day to trust myself and the choices that I make.

I am learning to accept what has happened to me, and I am feeling more at ease each day.

I understand that it is my choice if and when I forgive my assailant.

Each day the assailant has less control over me as I learn to have greater control over myself.

Although I will never be the same person I was before the attack, I am healing, growing, and recovering, and I will make it through this process a stronger person.

· ·

Reality Check:
There is no justification, either religious or otherwise, in believing that your rape is God's punishment.

· ·

Rape is not an act of God. It is an act of violence and intimidation, not only against a woman's body, but also against her very soul, regardless of her religious upbringing or affiliation.

This time of recovery can be a time to reflect inward. Pray, meditate, ask for peace of mind and the help that you need to heal.

What Friends and Family Can Do

Rape is a crime that has many victims. It affects not only the person who was raped, but also friends, lover, family, and anyone who is currently in a relationship with the victim or the rapist. The significant other's response to the survivor after the rape can be the most important factor in her healing. If you are involved with or related to a woman who has been raped, you may experience any or all of the following emotions:

Guilt: It is common for you to feel guilty for not being there to protect her.

Anger: Obviously, you will be angry at the rapist, but taking the law into your own hands and rushing out to get the guy is not what she needs right now. She has enough to worry about without wondering if you are going to get killed or put in jail. Your rage against the rapist may be interpreted by her as anger or violence against her as well.

Depression: You, like she, may get depressed at the incident because it has changed both of your lives forever. She may withdraw from you and seem to change. This is normal. You may want your relationship to go back to the way it was as quickly as possible. This is unrealistic and unfair. It also places blame upon her because she can't get beyond the incident according to your timetable. Give her time!

Denial: You may react by pointing out that she did not get hurt, so why can't she just forget about it? This attempt to minimize her pain will only make her feel more isolated from you and the world, as well as tell her that you really do not understand what she is going through. She may really need to talk it through—let her.

Disbelief: You may not believe everything she tells you about the incident. Maybe she did not act the way you think she should have or maybe she was not physically beaten to the degree that there are bruises. If you do not believe her, it will only harm her. She needs your unconditional support right now. Do not hold back. If you have trouble understanding her, her story, and the way she's reacting to you, contact a rape crisis counselor who can give you some insight into her condition.

Overprotection: You may want to take control of her life, never leave her alone, etc. Remember, she has just gone through a situation in which her control was taken away from her. She needs to feel that you will protect her but will also encourage her to take control of her life again.

What She Needs from You

The journey from pain takes time and involves releasing fears. She can grow in spite of her pain if she gets support. Be patient with her moods, never give up on her, and accept her own unique way of dealing with her trauma. Ultimately, this experience can be used as a means to change her life for the better, depending on how she looks at it, but for now, allow her the time to heal without your time limits or your expectations. Give yourself time to heal as well. Be honest in your own needs and avoid denial; it only leads to emotional blocks.

You may need professional help in order to understand and cope with the aftermath of rape. Here is how you can best support your friend or loved one:

Believe her. Regardless of the circumstances, if she feels that she has been raped, then she has been. Do not question her, even if her story does not make sense. She may be withholding details in order not to upset you.

She has just been through a brush with death, and that is bound to have an effect on her.

Reassure her. She needs to know that what she is feeling is normal for someone who has been raped. She is bound to have many confusing feelings right now. Tell her it's okay, that it's going to take time for her to recover. Express some of your own feelings as well. It will give her permission to share what she is feeling.

Listen to her. Hear what she is really saying about herself. Do not close the door on what has happened before she is ready. Every rape survivor responds differently to the assault, and individual recovery time varies. Trying to minimize the attack's impact on her will isolate her and drive her away from you. Be patient.

Let her know how you feel. Share your feelings with her as well as with a rape crisis counselor or therapist. Don't tell her, "I understand," or, "I know how you feel," unless you have been victimized by rape yourself. You can't know how she feels. Just listen and be there for her.

Don't take control. It is normal to want to rescue her, to protect her, to surround her with your presence. Be patient. Reassure her that you will be there as much as she needs, but that you know she is capable of making decisions and being in control of her own life. Besides, you can't be there all the time for her. Her independence should always be encouraged.

Patience, patience, patience. Don't expect too much from her. Her ability to recover and the length of time it will take depends on you, her family, the kind of help she gets, and her self-esteem prior to the rape. Understand that if your sexual relationship changes, this is normal. She may take her anger out on you. On a subconscious or conscious level, she may put you in the same category as the rapist. She may feel that all men are the same. Keep telling her, "I'm on your side," and, "I know you're angry, I'm angry too." Encourage her to get professional help and agree to get help with her. Although you were not the one who was raped, you both need to deal with the stress the rape places on your relationship. In fact, you both were victimized by the rapist. There is nothing wrong with getting help for yourself with a therapist or a professional counselor.

Sexual Assault: Harassment, Stalking, Dating, and Domestic Violence

Chapter Thirteen

Sexual Harassment

Date and acquaintance rape often starts as a series of intimidations and manipulations of a sexual nature. This is called sexual harassment, and it can be a confusing issue today, but you should understand that you can be harassed regardless of your age or appearance. Many women have experienced sexual harassment, and the law is beginning to address this area.

Sexual harassment is a form of sex discrimination that violates Title VII of the Civil Rights Act of 1964, as amended. It is defined by the Equal Employment Opportunity Commission as unwelcome sexual advances, requests for sexual favors, and other verbal or physical conduct of a sexual nature when submission to or rejection of this conduct (1) explicitly or implicitly affects an individual's employment, (2) unreasonably interferes with an individual's work performance, or (3) creates an intimidating, hostile, or offensive work environment. U.S. law recognizes two types of sexual harassment. The first is termed *quid pro quo*, Latin for "this for that," implying a trade involving sex (e.g., a supervisor offering a subordinate a promotion in exchange for sexual favors or denying a job benefit because of refusal of the supervisor's advances). The second type is "hostile environment" harassment, which is less blatant and harder to define. This occurs when an employee is placed in an uncomfortable or threatening environment due to unwelcome sexual behavior in the workplace. Examples of hostile environment situations include telling jokes or stories of a sexual nature; unwelcome touching, such as patting or hugging; displaying suggestive or sexually explicit photographs, posters, or calendars; or making suggestive facial expressions or gestures.

There are Three Forms of Sexual Harassment:

Verbal harassment, such as epithets, derogatory jokes or comments, slurs or unwanted sexual advances, and invitations or comments. Examples range from regularly referring to others with inconsiderate terms and compliments, such as: "Hey baby," "honey," remarks about ones body or clothes, sexual jokes; nicknames; asking someone out that has already turned you down; sexual invitations and more. These may be in person or via voice mail, email, or other recordings.

Visual harassment includes offensive, derogatory and/or sexually-oriented posters, pictures, cartoons, emails, and drawings; reading sexual magazines in the workplace; viewing pornography and sexually explicit or derogatory web sites; or making sexual gestures. Although it can be difficult to determine what is appropriate at work, these types of materials should not be in the workplace. When an employee is exposed to these things at work, the exposure can create an intimidating, hostile, or offensive working environment.

Physical harassment includes assault, unwanted touching, blocking normal movement, or interfering with work. Examples include intentionally brushing up against someone, caressing or massaging the person's shoulders, cornering someone so that person has to talk or listen to you, sitting on the desk to impede your work or get someone's attention, grabbing, holding, or touching another person in any way that is unwelcome, including assault and rape.

Outrageous But True Figures

50 to 80 percent of women in the workplace experience sexual harassment at least once in their careers

15 percent of complaints filed are by men

95 percent of all such incidents may not be reported

A typical Fortune 500 corporation can expect to lose $10 million annually from absenteeism, lower productivity, increased health-care costs, poor morale, and employee turnover as a result of sexual harassment

Sexual harassment victims can recover compensatory damages beyond back pay, future pecuniary losses, emotional pain, suffering, inconvenience, mental anguish, loss of enjoyment of life, and punitive damages, and may do so in a jury trial

Over $150 million was awarded to victims of sexual harassment in the United States in 1999

(National Organization of Women Website.)

According to a *USA Today* report, "Although it can be a precursor to acts of violence and other criminal acts, sexual harassment is not itself legally classified as a crime in most jurisdictions in the United States; therefore, it can be addressed only through a civil action."[15]

Sexual harassment is unwanted, repeated sexual attention. Not only is it offensive, it's against civil law. Sexual harassment is illegal even if the harasser is not your boss, your professor, or your teacher. It is illegal even if the perpetrator is not overtly stating to you that you will lose your job or your academic standing if you don't go along with his sexual contacts. It also is illegal if the harassment creates a hostile or offensive environment that interferes with your ability to do your job or continue your academic pursuits.

Here are some behaviors that the law may deem to be sexual harassment:

- Slurs or abuse
- Sexual innuendoes and other suggestive, offensive, or derogatory comments
- Humor and jokes about sex (or gender-specific traits)
- Sexist remarks about your body, clothing, or sexual activity
- Sexual propositions or subtle pressure for sexual activities
- Insults of a sexual nature
- Requests or demands for sexual favors
- Catcalls

- Leering, ogling, whistling
- Suggestive or insulting sounds or gestures
- Use of inappropriate body images to advertise events
- Visual displays of degrading sexual images
- Unnecessary and unwanted physical contact (e.g., touching, brushing, pinching)
- Attempts to impede or block movement
- Attempted or actual fondling or kissing
- Physical assault or coerced sexual intercourse

The basic point to remember is that sexual harassment is unwanted, unsolicited, or undesired attention of a sexual nature. Sexual harassment is a breach of the trusting relationship that normally exists between the employer and employee, or between the professor and student. Boundaries between the professional role and the personal relationship blur because the harasser intrudes into what should be a sex-neutral situation. Sexual harassment can escalate into rape.

· ·

Reality Check:
Sexual harassment is not about sex—it's about power.
Typically, such behavior is designed to humiliate and control.

· ·

Both males and females can be victims or perpetrators of sexual harassment, although as with other types of sexual assault, the majority of harassment is perpetrated by men against women. More than half, and perhaps as many as two-thirds, of sexual harassment cases recorded by the Equal Employment Opportunity Commission involve male perpetrators and female victims.[16]

Hostile Environment
In a hostile environment claim, the complainant must demonstrate that a reasonable person would find the working environment hostile and abusive, and that she herself was offended, a requirement easily met where the

offending conduct has affected psychological well-being in a demonstra-ble way. Even without serious psychological injury, the employee may still show that the conduct was offensive. If, however, she herself contributed by speech or actions to a sexually charged atmosphere, the employee may be unable to show that her complaint is legitimate.

In addition, not all conduct of a sexual nature in the workplace is unlawful. The touchstone of whether harassment has occurred is whether the challenged conduct is unwelcome. The courts have stated that an iso-lated comment will not constitute harassment. Rather, the totality of the circumstances must be considered, including the frequency and severity of the offending conduct, whether it is physically threatening or humiliating, and whether it unreasonably interferes with the employee's performance.

Current law does not require that a victim of sexual harassment first make an internal complaint before filing a claim. However, if the employ-er has a complaint procedure that encourages victims to come forward, failure to complain may undercut efforts to show that the employee was offended. If the employer has no complaint procedure, or if the procedure would require the victim to report the complaint to the harasser, then the lack of complaint won't affect the employee's case.

How to Prevent or Deal with Sexual Harassment

Sexual harassment is illegal, and most corporate and school policies pro-hibit any employee or student from engaging in sexual harassment.

Speak up at the time of the perceived harassment situation: Say "no!" clearly, firmly, and without smiling. This is not the time to be polite or vague. Inform the harasser that his attentions are unwanted. Make clear that you find the behavior offensive. By being quiet, you enable the harass-ment to continue. Speaking up can protect others from being victimized and may decrease your feelings of helplessness. If you have clearly requested that the behavior stop and it doesn't, write a memo to the harasser and keep a copy in your files.

Document the harassment. Write down each incident including date, time, and place. Detail what happened and include your response. Keep a copy at home. This information will be useful if you need to take legal action.

Document your work. Keep copies of performance evaluations and memos that attest to the quality of your work. The harasser may question your job performance in order to justify his behavior.

Look for witnesses and other victims. You are probably not the first person who has been mistreated by this individual. Ask around—you may find others who will support your charge. Two accusations are much harder to ignore. Don't be too disappointed if you find that other women who have been harassed are willing to ignore it—these people may be afraid for their jobs or have become so used to the offensive behavior that it doesn't bother them anymore. Sexual harassment will continue if good people do nothing.

Explore university and company channels. Use any grievance procedures or channels detailed in your employee handbook. If you are in a union, get the union steward involved right away.

Seek advice. This can help you determine whether what you are experiencing is sexual harassment and can provide help in preventing initial overtures from developing into harassment. You may begin by seeking advice from your human resources department, your union representative, your dean of students, or from an attorney or legal service. You do not need an attorney to file a sexual harassment claim, but before filing a claim, you may want to speak with a legal service or private attorney specializing in employment discrimination. For information on where to seek advice, call 9 to 5, an advocacy organization of working women. Several of their chapters have formed sexual harassment support groups. Their toll-free number is (800) 522-0925.

File a complaint. If you need to pursue a legal remedy, contact your state discrimination agency or the federal Equal Employment Opportunity Commission (Look in your telephone directory for the field office closest to you. The federal agency covers workplaces of fifteen or more people. State law may protect you if you're in a smaller workplace).

Don't blame yourself. Sexual harassment is unwanted action that the harasser decides to take. It is not your fault.

Don't delay. If you delay action, the harassment is likely to continue.

If You Observe Sexual Harassment

If you are an observer of what you perceive to be sexual harassment, you can take steps to stop this form of discrimination. You can

- Speak up. Inform the harasser that his/her actions may be perceived as sexual harassment.
- Support the victim. Provide comfort and assurances to the victim.
- Report the incident to appropriate persons within your office or school.

A final word about sexual harassment and standing up for yourself; I have seen and heard from hundreds of women who have put up with harassing and abusive behavior on a daily basis in the workplace. In most cases, I hear their pain and frustration, but also their weakness in not wanting to report their manager or coworker for the abuse. They eventually have to quit because they can't take it anymore. The larger tragedy here is that the company is never forced to change because everyone keeps silent. Corporations will never change unless they're forced into it. Keeping silent only ensures that the abusive behavior will continue to create more victims. Stand up for yourself. If you don't, who will?

New Liability for Schools

Historically, if one student harassed another, the school itself could not be sued or held responsible. This appears to be changing. In a Georgia case brought before the U.S. Supreme Court in 1999, a young girl had been continually harassed in school and, despite her mother's complaints, the school had done nothing to assist her. The mother sued the school, and the Court ruled that a school can be sued in civil court for not stopping one student from harassing another if the conduct has been reported to the school. This makes schools directly responsible to take action against sexual harassment between students, once the harassment is brought to the school's attention. This case has removed the immunity from lawsuits that schools have historically enjoyed and left schools throughout the country scrambling to formulate policies and procedures to prevent and otherwise deal with sexual harassment issues.

If you are still experiencing harassment, contact one of the following organizations:

General:

Equal Rights Advocates 1-800-839-4ERA www.equalrights.org

NOW Legal Defense and Education Fund 212-925-6635 www.nowl-def.org

National Women's Law Center: 202-588-5180 www.nwlc.org

In the Workplace:

9-5 National Association of Working Women 1-800-522-0925 www.9to5.org

Equal Employment Opportunity Commission

In California: 415-356-5100 or 510-637-3230 www.eeoc.gov

California Department of Fair Employment and Housing 1-800-884-1684 www.dfeh.ca.gov

Employment Law Center (Worker's Rights Clinics) 415-864-8208 www.las-elc.org

Nolo Press www.nolo.com A website to help people through the legal system. Includes access to online legal encyclopedia, legal dictionary, and legal research center.

At School:

Office of Civil Rights, U.S. Department of Education www.ed.gov/offices/OCR

Chapter Fourteen

Stalking

Probably the most insidious of all sexual crimes is that of stalking—the never-ending control, manipulation, and pursuit of the intended victim. In general, it is such a heinous crime that the stalker rarely ends his pursuit until either he or the victim is dead.

Primarily state statutes legally define stalking. While statutes may vary from state to state, most define stalking as a course of conduct that places a person in fear for personal safety. The variety of specific strategies employed and behaviors displayed by stalkers are limited only by the creativity and ingenuity of the stalkers themselves. In other words, virtually any unwanted contact between a stalker and his victim, which directly or indirectly communicates a threat or places the victim in fear, can generally be referred to as stalking.

Stalking is not a new phenomenon. Until recently, it was not labeled as a separate and distinct class of deviant behavior, but was referred to as harassment, annoyance, or, in some cases, simply as domestic violence. In the 1980s and 1990s, numerous high-profile cases involving celebrities began to catch the attention of the media and public policy leaders. Only then did such behavior begin to be described as "stalking." Stalking has now become a common subject in the popular media. With blockbuster films such as *Fatal Attraction*, *Cape Fear*, and *Sleeping with the Enemy*—and their coverage by the news media—stalking has become a household word.

Until recently, law enforcement officials did not track the incidences of stalking offenses as part of their normal crime reporting process. Since there has been virtually no empirical data available, no one knows just how common stalking cases are in the United States.

According to reliable estimates, as many as one of every twelve American women (8.2 million) and one of every forty-five American men (2 million) have been stalked at some point or other in their lives.[17] Seventy-eight percent of stalking victims are female, whereas 87 percent of stalkers are male. The first anti-stalking law was passed in California in 1990. With the passage of the 1994 Crime Bill by the U.S. Congress mandating the tracking and compilation of stalking crime statistical figures, experts are beginning to determine more accurately the prevalence of this crime.

Fifty-three percent of stalking cases are reported to the police.
About 12 percent of all stalking cases result in criminal prosecution.
About a quarter of female stalking victims and about a tenth of male stalking victims obtain restraining orders against their stalkers.
Sixty-nine percent of women and 81 percent of men with restraining orders said their stalkers violated the order.

The Two Types of Stalkers

There are two types of stalkers. Going by the statistical figures, it is evident that both females and males can be victims or perpetrators. Usually stalkers are men, however, and they are generally more violent than female stalkers. Figures indicate that 75 to 80 percent of all stalking cases are men stalking women.[18] Most stalkers are in the young to middle-age range, have above-average intelligence, and may come from any cultural and socio-economic background.[19]

Unfortunately, there is no single psychological or behavioral profile for stalkers. In fact, many experts believe that every stalker is unique, making it very difficult not only to categorize their behavior, but doubly difficult to devise effective strategies to cope with such behavior. Forensic psychol ogists, who study criminal behavior, are only beginning to examine the minds and motives of stalkers. These psychologists have identified two broad categories of stalkers and stalking behavior—"Love Obsession" and "Simple Obsession."

Love Obsession Stalker

This category is characterized by stalkers who seem to develop a love obsession for or fixation on another person with whom they have no personal relationship. The target may be only a casual acquaintance or even a complete stranger. This category represents about 20 to 25 percent of all stalking cases.

Those who stalk celebrities and stars—such as David Letterman, Jodie Foster, and Madonna—fall into the category of love obsessionists, but stalkers in this category also include those who develop fixations on regular, ordinary people including coworkers, casual acquaintances, or people they pass in the street.

The vast majority of love obsession stalkers seem to suffer from a mental disorder—often schizophrenia or paranoia. Regardless of the specific disorder, nearly all display some delusional thought patterns and behaviors. Since most are unable to develop normal personal relationships through more conventional and socially acceptable means, they retreat to lives of fantasy relationships with persons they hardly know. They apparently invent fictional stories—complete with what to them are real-life scripts—which cast their unwilling victims in the lead role as their own love interest. They then attempt to act out their fictional plots in the real world.

The woman who stalked talk show host David Letterman for years truly believed that she was his wife. She was discovered on Mr. Letterman's property numerous times, was arrested driving his car, and had even appeared at his residence with her own child in tow—each time insisting that she was David Letterman's wife. Not only do love-obsessional stalkers attempt to live out their fantasies, but they appear to expect their victims to play their assigned roles as well. They seem to believe that they can make the object of their affection love them. They desperately want to establish a positive personal relationship with their victim. When the victim refuses to follow the script or doesn't respond as the stalker hopes, the stalker may attempt to force the victim to comply by use of threats and intimidation. When threats and intimidation fail, some stalkers turn to violence. Some decide that if they cannot be a positive part of their victim's life, they will be part of their life in a negative way—sometimes even going so far as to murder their victims in twisted attempts to romantically link themselves to their victims forever. This was the case with the man who shot and killed Rebecca Schaffer, the young actress and star of the 1980s television sitcom *My Sister Sam*.

Simple Obsession Stalker

This second category represents 70 to 80 percent of all stalking cases and is distinguished by the fact that some previous personal or romantic relationship existed between the stalker and the victim before the stalking behavior began. Virtually all domestic violence cases involving stalking fall under this umbrella, as do casual dating relationships (commonly referred to by law enforcement agents as "Fatal Attraction" cases, named after the popular movie by the same title).

Whereas this kind of stalker may or may not have psychological disorders, all stalkers who have been examined clearly have personality disorders. One forensic psychologist has attempted to identify some of the common personality traits and behavioral characteristics among this category of stalker. Stalkers in this class are characterized as individuals who are

- Socially maladjusted and inept
- Emotionally immature
- Often subject to feelings of powerlessness
- Unable to succeed in relationships by socially acceptable means
- Jealous, bordering on paranoid
- Extremely insecure about themselves and suffering from low self-esteem

The self-esteem of simple obsession stalkers is often tied closely to their relationship with their partner. In many cases, such stalkers bolster their own self-esteem by dominating and intimidating their mates. Since the victim literally becomes the stalker's primary source of self-esteem, the stalker's greatest fear becomes the loss of this person. The stalker's own self-worth is so closely tied to the victim that when he is deprived of that person, he may feel that his own life is worthless. This is what makes simple obsession stalkers so dangerous. In the most extreme cases, these stalkers will stop at nothing to regain their "lost possession"—their partner—and in so doing, regain their lost self-esteem.

Simple-obsession stalkers are the most dangerous when they are deprived of their source of power and self-esteem—the relationship. This is the common thread in most domestic violence cases. Indeed, stalking cases that emerge from domestic violence situations constitute the most common and potentially lethal class of stalking cases.

If you are attempting to break off a relationship with a simple obsession stalker, he will desperately connive ways to get the relationship restarted. If you resist him or don't cooperate, he may use force or intimidation. If threats and intimidation fail, he may turn to violence. He cannot be objective about his ex-partner. He has only one desire, and that is to return to what he felt was the perfect relationship. He may define himself through that relationship and feel like a failure if the relationship fails. His violence may escalate to homicide from an obsessive belief that if he cannot have his victim in this life, then he will have her in the next.

Stalking Behavior Patterns

Stalking behavior patterns are in many ways similar to domestic violence. Much of the behavior is initiated when the stalker's attempts to control the victim are resisted. This happens during a relationship breakup as well as in the initial stages of a new relationship. The stalker may try to control his victim by sending flowers, candy, love letters, or expensive gifts. If she doesn't cooperate and return his affection, he may turn to intimidation. He may start by being jealous and wishing to have control over everything she does and everyone she sees.

There are basically three steps or stages in a stalking situation. If you recognize this behavior pattern in your life, either as a perpetrator or as a victim, you should seek professional help immediately.

The stalker's thoughts often progress from, "If I can just prove to you how much I love you!" to, "I can make you love me!" to, "If I can't have you, nobody else will!"

This progression in a stalker's thinking process is common; however, we cannot as yet predict a stalker's behavior. Some stalkers may threaten and intimidate at any point. Every stalking situation is different, and there is no one way to respond to a stalker's behavior that will prevent an escalation of violence.

Stalking and the Law

The first anti-stalking law was passed in California in 1990. In 1992, the U.S. Congress enacted legislation that required the attorney general, through the National Institute of Justice, to conduct research on the issue of stalking and to develop and distribute among the states a "constitutional and enforceable" model anti-stalking code.[20]

As of September 1993, all fifty states and the District of Columbia had some form of anti-stalking law. In 1996, the U.S. Congress passed the first federal anti-stalking law. Beyond a basic definition of the crime, statutes include a wide variety of additional stalking-related provisions. For example, some state stalking statutes

- Allow police to make arrests without a warrant in stalking cases where probable cause exists
- Make stalking a nonbailable offense under certain circumstances
- Provide for automatic and emergency protective orders
- Require mandatory psychological evaluation and treatment for stalkers
- Establish sentencing enhancements in cases where the victim is a minor, or when there is a protective order in place against the perpetrator
- Create heightened crime classifications for stalkers who commit multiple stalking offenses

Until anti-stalking legislation was enacted in most states, victims had few alternatives. Most laws passed previously had not given adequate protection to victims of stalking because they were intended to prosecute the stalker after he had already committed the crime. Watching, following, and intimidating another person was rarely taken seriously until physical damage had been committed. The only recourse available to women was to take out a restraining order. This rarely had any effect because restraining orders were designed to control the behavior of rational individuals who did not wish to commit a crime and go to jail. In essence, they were designed for people who had respect for the court's authority.

In most cases, a stalker is not coherent enough to understand or care about what the court orders and tends to be out of touch with reality.

For these reasons, legislators across the nation have implemented stalking legislation that protects individuals from stalkers. Anti-stalking legislation makes it a crime to engage in a pattern of behavior that harasses and/or threatens other people.

Three Types of Anti-stalking Laws

Generally, anti-stalking laws can be classified into three different categories related to penalties:

1. Those that make stalking a misdemeanor
2. Those that make a first offense of stalking a misdemeanor and subsequent offenses felonies
3. Those that make stalking a felony

For additional information about your state's anti-stalking laws, contact

Your state Attorney General's office
Your local prosecutor's office or law enforcement agency
Your local law library, or the reference librarian in your local library

Statutes that establish new crimes such as stalking are not universally implemented or instantaneously enforced from the moment they take effect. There is often a considerable lag time in implementing new statutes while law enforcement officials, prosecutors, and judges become familiar with the laws and develop policies and procedures to implement them.

Since stalking laws are fairly new, victims cannot always be certain that law enforcement officials, prosecutors, or even judges are aware of these new laws. Stalking victims may find it necessary to provide law enforcement officials with a copy of their state anti-stalking statute, along with evidence that proves that the stalker has violated the statute. Copies of such statutes can be found in your state's published criminal code, available in some public libraries and in all law libraries.

Preventing and Dealing with Stalking

If you are a victim of stalking, you must document all contact with the stalker, no matter how insignificant. The court will look at the conduct of the stalker and consider whether his behavior is reasonable or unreasonable. The court will take into consideration a victim's feelings and how much fear the stalker has caused through his actions. A complaint must be accompanied with sufficient evidence to establish "probable cause" that the stalker engaged in conduct that is illegal under the state's anti-stalking statute. If law enforcement officials do not witness such conduct firsthand, it is often up to the victim to provide them with the evidence necessary to establish probable cause.

You must be familiar with your state's anti-stalking law to know whether your stalker is indeed breaking the law. In Georgia, for example, a stalker cannot be prosecuted if he is watching you from his own residence. For instance, if a man is stalking you in your apartment complex, and he lives there as well, then the law would say that he had a right to be there. Georgia law also states that, if he is in the course of doing his job, i.e., if he is a police officer on duty, or a journalist pursuing a story, he can't be prosecuted.

In order to gain a clear understanding of what conduct constitutes an offense under your state's statute, you can obtain a copy of the statute from your local law library. You also can find a listing of each state's anti-stalking laws in the internet section of the "Resources" at the back of this book. You may wish to consult with law enforcement officials, prosecutors, or a private attorney for an explanation and interpretation of the specific stalking statute in question.

In other words, stalking victims are often put in a position of having first to prove their case to a law enforcement official before being afforded the opportunity to prove their case before a court of law.

For this reason it is crucial for stalking victims to
- Document every stalking incident as thoroughly as possible.
- Collect and keep any and all videotapes, audiotapes, answering machine messages, photos of the stalker, notes, letters, objects received from the stalker, eyewitness affidavits, and records of property damage.
- Keep a journal to document all contacts and incidents, along with the time, date, and other relevant information such as location, anyone else present, any conversation that took place, etc.

Regardless of whether or not they have sufficient evidence to prove a stalking violation, victims wishing to file a stalking complaint with law enforcement officials should do so at the earliest possible point in time. In some cases, victims may also be able to file a complaint in the jurisdiction where the offender resides if it is different from the victim's.

If law enforcement officials refuse to investigate, or if they are not responsive to a complaint filed, victims may directly approach their local prosecutor (also known in various jurisdictions as the district attorney, state's attorney, commonwealth's attorney, or state solicitor).

If you believe you are being stalked, seek assistance from the local domestic violence agency or rape crisis center. They have trained staff who can help you develop a personal safety plan in case you need it to escape.

The following information is a set of general actions you can take if you choose. Of course, your first step should always be to contact your local law enforcement agency.

If You Are in Imminent Danger

If you are in imminent danger, your primary goal should be to locate a safe place for yourself. Safety for stalking victims can often be found in the following places:
- Police stations
- Residences of family/friends that are unknown to the stalker
- Domestic violence shelters or local churches
- Public areas (stalkers may be less inclined toward violence or creating a disturbance in public places).

If departure from your current location is not possible, but a telephone is accessible, contact local law enforcement at 9-1-1 or any other law enforcement or emergency number. If the police do not indicate that they are sending an officer to you immediately, ask to speak to the police unit or division supervisor.

In dangerous situations, family members or friends can assist you in departing from your home or office. Always exercise caution, as stalking sometimes escalates into violence.

Upon reaching safety, you may want to communicate with law enforcement, victim services, mental health professionals and/or social services agencies in order to receive additional assistance and referrals available in your community. As a victim of stalking, you always should identify yourself as such and request confidentiality of all information given and any records kept or filed. If the stalker caused property damage or physical harm, you may choose to file a report with law enforcement immediately.

If You Are in Danger, but Not Immediately at Risk

If you determine that you are at risk for being in a potentially harmful or violent situation, the following options may be considered:

Restraining/Protective/Stay-Away Orders. Generally, these orders require the offender to stay away from—and not interfere with—the complainant. Violation of such orders may be punishable by incarceration, a fine, or both. These orders are typically obtained through a magistrate's office or local court. Contact the local Clerk of Court's office for information about where to obtain orders.

* * *

Reality Check:

Restraining orders are not foolproof—often they do not
extend beyond certain lines of jurisdiction, and
they can be enforced only if they are broken. Be careful
not to develop a false sense of security.

* * *

In addition, some states provide protective orders only to former spouses or intimates. Moreover, it often costs money to obtain such an order based on filing fees, or in some courts and jurisdictions, based on the need to obtain legal assistance. Orders are not guaranteed—they are at the court's discretion.

Police Notification. If the perpetrator has broken the law by entering your residence without your permission, stealing and/or destroying your property, physically and/or sexually assaulting you, these acts may be punishable. Notifying police of illegal acts are important because: (1) if convicted, the perpetrator may be incarcerated and/or ordered to stay away from you; (2) charges may intimidate the offender, sending the message that his/her actions are illegal and will not be tolerated; and (3) filing a charge produces documentation, which may be useful in a future complaint for evidentiary or credibility purposes.

Documentation. Documentation of stalking should be saved and given to law enforcement personnel. Documentation of the actions of the perpetrator may be useful in future complaints or proceedings, for evidentiary or credibility purposes. Documentation may take the form of photos of destroyed property/vandalism, photos of any injuries inflicted by the perpetrator, answering machine messages saved on tape, letters or notes written by the perpetrator, etc. You should keep a written log of any crimes or suspicious activities committed by the perpetrator. Use discretion when making entries, as the log may be used in court proceedings. Keep the log in a safe and secure location.

Contingency Plans. Although you may not be in imminent danger, the potential for harm always exists; therefore, a contingency plan may be appropriate. You may wish to keep a small packed suitcase in the trunk of your car or at another readily accessible location in case you decide against going home, or in case you need to depart your home suddenly.

Make sure you have access to critical telephone numbers, including
• Law enforcement numbers and locations
• Safe places (such as friends, domestic violence shelters, etc.)
• Contact numbers for use after safety is secured (such as neighbors or family, attorneys, prosecutors, medical care, child care, pet care, etc.). Reserve money may be necessary. Some stalkers have the means of

ruining your credit and tying up your finances. You may need to have a financial reserve.

Keep other necessities with you, such as creditors' telephone numbers and personal welfare items such as medication, birth certificates, social security information, passports, etc.

Miscellaneous Items. Always keep as full a tank of gas as possible in your car, and provide backup keys for neighbors. Inform people about your situation who may be useful in formulating a contingency plan, such as: law enforcement; employers; family, friends, or neighbors; and security personnel.

Nine Ways to Deal with Stalking

1. Install solid core doors with dead bolts in your home. If you cannot account for all keys, change the locks immediately and secure any and all spare keys.

2. Install adequate lighting outside your house . Trim back bushes and vegetation around your residence. Your lighting should shine out, away from the house. You can purchase motion-sensor lights that will come on when someone enters your property. Some of these lights also will signal interior lights to go on, alerting you that someone has penetrated your perimeter.

3. Maintain an unlisted phone number. If harassing calls persist, notify local law enforcement, but also keep a written log of harassing calls and of any answering machine tapes of calls with the stalker's voice and messages. If you have the financial means, use a "dummy" answering machine connected to a published phone line. The number to a private unlisted line can be reserved for close friends and family—the stalker never may realize that you have another telephone line.

4. Treat any threats as legitimate and inform law enforcement immediately.

5. Vary your travel routes, and the stores, restaurants, etc., that you use regularly. Limit time walking and jogging. You might have to walk/jog with a male friend or exercise indoors or at a club where access is limited.

6. Inform a trusted neighbor and/or colleagues about the situation. Provide the friend with a photo or description of the suspect and of any vehicles he drives.

7. If residing in an apartment with an on-site property manager, provide the manager with a picture of the suspect. It is important to understand that if the stalker also lives in the apartment complex, you cannot, in most cases, file a stalking report against him in that area, because he has the right to be there.

8. Have coworkers screen all calls and visitors.

9. When out of the house or work environment, try not to travel alone if at all possible, and try to stay in public areas. If you ever need assistance, yell "fire" to get immediate attention, because people respond more readily to this cry for assistance than to any other.

Do not assume that if your stalker is arrested and goes to jail that he will leave you alone. There are numerous cases of stalkers who are sent to prison for many years, and who after their release, find their obsession and kill her. Remember that you are not dealing with a rational human being. Never assume you can reason with him and get him to permanently leave you alone.

How to Find the Source of Secretive Phone Calls

Continuous, secretive, obscene, or harassing phone calls can be very scary and stressful. Even if calls are not threatening they can be of great inconvenience. However, there are various options available to you to put an end to these calls. In most cases, simply uncloaking the individual is enough to bring your problems to swift and successful resolution.

What type of phone calls are generally considered to be harassing?
When someone calls and uses obscene or threatening language.
When someone calls repeatedly and hangs up.
When someone calls and breathes heavy or remains silent to intimidate you.

How often do I have to get these calls to consider it as harassment?
Generally any unwelcome call is harassing; however, your telephone company or local law enforcement will not take any action unless calls are frequent. If the caller threatens you or your family with bodily harm then the phone company or law enforcement will take prompt action.

What options do I have when I get harassing calls?
The first thing to do is to call your phone company. Different phone companies have different policies on whether you should call the phone company or the police first. Some phone companies may ask you to call the phone company's local office and explain the problem. Other phone companies may require that you file a formal complaint with local police before they will deal with the matter. You should contact your local phone company and find out what their policy is in matters of harassing calls. If the threats are serious and your life or your property is threatened, or if the obscene phone calls are very frequent, then you should call your local police immediately and file a report and provide all the details. You should also write down dates and times of calls and if the caller sounded male or female and what background noise, if any, you heard. If any phone number was displayed on your caller ID you should write that down, too.

What does it mean when sometimes my phone rings and there is no one on the line?
When you receive frequent hang ups on your phone line it could be that someone is checking to see if you are home or it is simply harassment. It could also be calls from telemarketers who use computers to call consumers. When someone answers, the computer finds a sales representative who is not occupied at that time and connects the call. If all sales reps are busy then consumer may hear only silence. This type of call is an "abandoned call." If you are receiving many abandoned calls in a day, you can call your local phone company to pursue options. If these repeated calls are from a malicious individual who is harassing you rather than a telemarketer, the phone company will generally report the number to law enforcement.

What options do I have to stop other kinds of unwanted calls?

To avoid unwanted calls you can ask your phone company what options they provide. Many companies offer screening options that allow you to refuse calls from certain numbers and block numbers when you are suffering from repeated hang ups. Most phone companies charge a monthly fee for this service. However, call screening services are not a foolproof way to stop unwelcome calls. A determined caller can move to a different phone number to bypass the block. You can try using call return (by dialing *69): This service allows you to call back the number of the last person who called, even if you are unable to answer the phone. Some people suggest that call return can be used to stop harassing callers by allowing you to call the harasser back without knowing their phone number. Use caution with this method of discouraging harassing callers, however, as it could actually aggravate the problem. This service is paid on a per-use basis.

You can use caller ID to identify the caller if they are not blocking their number or use a service offered by most phone companies called privacy manager. It works with caller ID to identify incoming calls that have no telephone numbers. Calls identified as anonymous, unavailable, out of the area or private must identify themselves in order to complete the call. Before your phone rings, a recorded message instructs the caller to unblock the call, enter a code number (like inbound call blocking devices mentioned above), or record their name. When your phone rings, you can choose to accept or reject the call, send it to voice mail, or send a special message to telemarketers instructing them to put you on their "do not call" list.

Cyber-Stalking

The internet and the World Wide Web have changed the way some women and men meet and develop relationships. Harassment can and does happen on the internet, and cyber-stalking is fast becoming a problem for women who are connected to the Web. The information in this section will give you some alternatives to protect your online privacy, and will explain what options are open to you if you want to prosecute an online stalker.

Harassment on the internet can be as threatening as any personal contact harassment. Just because you don't have a face-to-face stalking situation with the stalker doesn't mean that you won't be unnerved, frightened, and in potential danger. Internet harassment is not only unsolicited email, but any systematic and continually disturbing communication from an unwanted individual. Such contacts include

- Unwanted/unsolicited email
- Unwanted/unsolicited talk requests
- Private or public messages posted on newsgroups
- Disturbing messages on usenet newsgroups or bulletin boards
- Unsolicited communications about you to coworkers, friends, and acquaintances
- Off-line communication such as paper mail or phone calls

Some law enforcement agencies don't take reports of online harassment and stalking as a serious threat because they may believe that a woman can easily disconnect from the internet if she is receiving disturbing communication. This can be true, but it may not be possible to totally disconnect from the internet because of job requirements. It is also unreasonable to expect a woman to change her lifestyle so that the perpetrator can't get to her.

There are several ways to block unwanted communication; however, it is often impossible to block all unsolicited emails and online harassment.

· ·

Reality Check:
Harassment on the internet is just as illegal as harassment in person.

· ·

Cyber-Stalking Avoidance
Be cautious about with whom you communicate and what you reveal about yourself. The internet is a great communication tool. It is also an anonymous tool. Not everything you read in an email may be true. Many people lie about themselves during email conversations. Even if there's no

immediate threat of physical danger on the internet, you still have to be careful about the type of information you divulge. As with unsolicited telephone calls, you don't have to be nice to everyone, and you don't have to get into a conversation with everyone who demands your attention. Make it a practice not to answer unsolicited email or instant messages. If you feel at all uncomfortable with the conversation you're having with someone online, you have every right to stop all communication. Be even more careful whom you decide to meet in person. Friendships and professional relationships you start online can be beneficial relationships, but it's very difficult to predict what someone you have met online is like in person.

Reality Check:
Dating from an internet meeting can be very dangerous.
Many people lie about themselves in chat rooms.

Check your personal information that might be on the internet. This is stored in your user identification or attached to your name and address. Be careful of your personal information in filling out forms and credit applications. Be selective where you submit your name, address, phone number, picture, or work history. If you are looking for work, you increase your risk when you place your resume on the internet. This is especially true if your address and phone number is attached to your job application and resume. You should be consistently curious about what information is online and remove those things that can lead a cyber-stalker to your front door. If you are online and use the internet for email and other business and entertainment reasons, you need to be vigilant as to what kind of information you are making accessible to the public.

- Keep your user ID generic and guarded. Does your ID say that you are female?
- Change your signature file so that it does not contain personal information, such as your full name, address, workplace, or any of your phone numbers.

- Use the "Finger" Ultimate Directory (finger.com) on the internet, to check into the amount of personal information that is available to the public. If you think Finger reveals too much about you, edit your file so that your privacy is protected.
- If you have a website, does it contain a photo, a resume, your name, address, work or home phone numbers; or does it list information about friends, family, or the area where you live? Such information should be limited in scope.
- In your browser's HTML editor, you can check your web page source code to make sure registration information (such as your name) hasn't been inserted automatically by your HTML editor.
- Be cautious about posting information to internet directories, bulletin boards, and other websites.
- Be your own private detective and investigate internet search engines (Alta Vista, Yahoo, Excite, etc., Usenet directories, and 4-1-1 phone directories) for your name.
- Could someone conceivably link your phone directory information to your online information and find out where you live? Yes. Technology is advancing so rapidly that there is no guarantee that your phone number will not give someone your address, as well as other private information. There are sites on the internet that will give a stalker your address, phone number, social security number, and even an unlisted cell phone number for as little as $7.95.
- Once you have done your online homework, you can program your browser to eliminate personal information being transferred during your connections to the Web. Consult your browser's user manual or help file, or call their technical support department for instructions on how to program your particular browser.

Actions to Take

If you are getting unsolicited email, ignore it. If the online stalker doesn't get a response from you, he may choose another victim.

Demand, in writing, that your stalker cease and desist. Inform him that his communications are unwanted and inappropriate and that you will take further action if it does not stop. Don't worry about whether your letter sounds too harsh—make sure it's professional and to the point. Send the letter via registered mail. Make sure he has to sign for it and that you get back a written form that he received the letter. Put a copy of the letter you sent with the postal registration form in a safe place. If the stalking continues, have an attorney send a letter indicating that legal action will follow if the unwanted communication does not stop. After you send this mail, your communication with him must stop. Any further communication can feed his obsession. Remember that the harasser is looking for a sign from you that he is getting to you. Your attention to him is his reward and it will fuel his attempts to harass you. It is common in a court case of harassment and stalking for the defendant to indicate the communication was not one-sided but consensual. If you file a harassment or stalking case, you will be expected to prove that the communication was definitely one-sided and unsolicited.

Document everything. Documentation should include every piece of email or other form of communication from this person, including all of the header information from an email or newsgroup posting. Also document how each communication is affecting your life, and what steps you are taking to remedy the situation.

If you are getting chat requests from an Internet Relay Chat (IRC) room such as an AOL Instant Messenger, or any other type of communication, print it out, and write the date and time of the message. You might also indicate whether the message frightened you and how it affects you. Remember that the court will take into consideration how the communication affects the stalking victim. They will want to analyze whether the message is intimidating and how it is affecting your life. Before you file a complaint with the police, send copies of each harassing communication to your email's Webmaster and the harasser's email Webmaster. Each email server has a person who administers email traffic. Most email servers consider unsolicited emails and online harassment to be against their in-house ethical standards and will disconnect the harasser if he doesn't stop. This doesn't mean that he will stop, because he can easily get another email server, and as long as he has your email address or website, he can start harassing you again. In addition to your archive of communications, start a log that explains the situation in more detail. Document how the harassment is affecting your life, and document what steps you're taking to stop it.

Report the situation to your friends, family, and coworkers. Tell friends or coworkers not to communicate with the harasser in any way. Inform your system administrator, your supervisor and work security personnel, as well as your apartment building's security people.

Report the situation to your local police. The FBI will also accept a complaint, and they will follow up on it if they have the available resources. Many states have modified their anti-stalking laws to include electronic communications and will let you file a restraining order. You'll need the person's street address if you want to serve him with a restraining order or press charges against him. The police can get this information from the harasser's postmaster if they need to. The court may ask your harasser to reimburse you for any filing fees that you incurred if you win the case.

Change your password frequently. Pay attention to your files, directories, and last logout information. You may wish to stay out of any usenet or chat rooms that the stalker has frequented.

Remember that all harassment and stalking, whether via the internet or face-to-face, are potentially very dangerous. Assume the worst and take all necessary precautions as if your life depended on it.

My Space and other social networking sites on the internet present a convenient lure for many predators. The following information from the Los Angeles Police Department should be taken to heart.

In recent years, many free online social networking sites have come into existence and have become increasingly popular among minors, especially teenagers.

Estimates suggest that in addition to My Space and Facebook, there are more than two hundred social networking sites in existence; some of the most popular sites boast registrants numbering in the tens of millions, with hundreds of thousands of new registrants per day. These sites allow individuals to communicate with each other and to form networks. As a registrant of these sites, a member can create a profile that is a unique web page, established so that the member can identify himself or herself to others.

These websites allow their members to customize their profiles with features including a forum for outside viewers to access photographs and details about the member, including physical attributes and personal information, as well as to access comments and thoughts posted by the member. Viewers of the member's profile may also contact the member via email or instant messenger, unless restricted by the member from doing so.

National Initiative, and their counterpart law enforcement officers around the country, have reported the increased use of social networking sites by sex offenders who troll sites in order to locate and communicate with potential victims. The websites' popularity in developing new friendships makes it possible for sex offenders to seek victims by joining the site. Although some of these websites have specific age requirements in order to join, research has shown that minimally effective or nonexistent monitoring by both parents and website operators have made it possible for underage children to join.

The FBI has successfully fostered relationships with willing companies that operate social networking sites in efforts to aid law enforcement in the detection of online sexual predators, in addition to establishing a partnership that will contribute to a safer online environment.

This advisory should serve as a reminder to parents and legal guardians that their vigilance is necessary in monitoring the use of the internet by minors under their supervision. Some tips for parents or guardians are listed below:

- Monitor your teenager's use of the internet at all times. With regard to social networking sites, discuss safeguards with your child and explain the need for your involvement in setting up restrictions for access.
- Ensure your teenager is not misrepresenting his or her age while on the internet.
- Even if a minor does not post personal information on their profile, a predator may track him or her down by perusing the profile of one of his/her friends, on which your child might be featured.
- Read and exercise the safety tips listed on the site of which your teenager is a member, and report inappropriate behavior directly to the website.

- Place your teenager's computer in the family room to facilitate monitoring of online activity.
- Restrict your teenager's profiles and groups on social networking sites to people your child knows personally; do not allow access to individuals your child has met through the internet. Most sites allow for parents to block questionable individuals from contacting their children by viewing their child's profile.
- Children and teenagers should be discouraged from posting personal information.

The National Center for Missing and Exploited Children operates a CyberTipline at www.cybertipline.com that allows parents and children to report child pornography and other incidents of sexual exploitation of children by submitting an online form. Complaints received by NCMEC that indicate a violation of federal law are referred to the FBI for appropriate action. Violations of state or local law are referred to the appropriate authorities.

CONTACT
Laura Eimiller: 310-996-3343; Cathy Viray: 310 996-3804;
Lourdes Arocho: 310-996-4402 (Spanish Speaker)

Chapter Fifteen

Dating and Domestic Violence

Dating and domestic violence, such as rape, harassment, and stalking, are crimes of power and domination attributable to the same issues of male aggression. Violence inside an intimate relationship exists on a continuum of controlling behavior, ranging from verbal and emotional abuse to physical assault. In addition, this kind of violence is linked directly to the perpetrator having witnessed or experienced violence during his childhood. Batterers are everyday people of all races and socio-economic backgrounds.

Dating violence is a pattern of continual acts that threaten or physically or sexually abuse a partner while in a relationship.

Domestic violence is a pattern of continual acts that threaten or physically or sexually abuse a member of the abuser's household. This can be a spouse, ex-spouse, sibling, other relative, or resident of the home.

Dating violence and domestic violence both stem from the perpetrator's need for power and control and exist on a continuum of aggressive behaviors by the abuser. The dynamics of abuse and the victim's responses to the abuse are very similar in both dating and domestic violence situations.

In many cases, the only difference is that the victim of domestic violence is often economically dependent on the abuser. The victim may believe that she would be homeless and destitute without the financial support of the perpetrator. In dating violence situations, the victim is not generally dependent upon the abuser for shelter and financial support, but there may be a strong need for the financial or social benefits of being in an ongoing relationship with the abuser. Dating violence may begin as early as the teenage years. One in ten teenagers will experience some form of physical abuse in dating relationships.

Many young people come to believe that love and abuse in relationships go hand-in-hand, especially because they may have little else with which to compare their experiences. They may downplay the physical abuse of their partner by making excuses for him. They may think that abusive or jealous behaviors are signs that their partners love them. This is especially true if being in a relationship is the most important thing in a young person's life. Young people in junior high school and high school can be obsessed with being popular. Popularity at this time of life often means having a date, going steady, or being in a relationship. When abuse starts to occur, friends may not encourage the victim to get help, because they believe this kind of behavior is normal or because they are also in abusive relationships and need to cover up the abuse. Unless they are exposed to healthy relationships, victims of dating violence often suffer needlessly, without the realization that the abuse is not acceptable, not normal, and certainly not their fault.

The movement to protect victims of domestic violence has many supporters. There are numerous laws and improvements in law enforcement training for the protection of these victims. However, for those young girls experiencing dating violence, there is not much support. The normal options for a victim of domestic violence—restraining orders, injunctions, arrest of the abuser—generally are not available in a dating violence situation because the victim may not be considered by law enforcement officials to be in imminent danger.

The Pattern of Teen Dating Violence

Dating violence generally exhibits a pattern of behavior with these common elements:

• Repeated violence escalates into more abusive behavior.
• Violence increases in severity the longer the relationship continues.

- Violence and abusive behaviors are followed with apologies and promises to change.
- Terminating the relationship increases the threats and level of violence for the victim.

Many times, the controlling behavior of the abuser will isolate the victim from her friends and make the possibility of getting help more difficult. She may feel increasingly alone and confused about how to escape the abuser. Teenagers in a dating violence situation may be reluctant to seek help from adults. They may distrust adults and be afraid of interference in the relationship. They also may be afraid that whatever independence they have will be taken away from them if they can't handle their own problems.

Though drugs and alcohol do play a part in abuse, they are not the cause of the abuse. They may be an excuse, but they are not the reason for the abuse.

Fifteen Warning Signs of Dating Violence

1. The man gets too serious about the relationship too quickly.
2. He is jealous and possessive, won't let you have friends, checks up on you, and won't accept breaking up.
3. He tries to control you by being very bossy, giving orders, and making all the decisions.
4. He humiliates you and belittles your opinions.
5. You are frightened of him and worry about how he will react to things you say or do.
6. He threatens you.
7. He is violent, has a history of fighting, loses his temper quickly, or brags about mistreating others. He may use or own weapons.
8. He pressures you for sex, or forces you to do sexual things that you don't want to do. He may attempt to manipulate you or lay a guilt-trip on you by saying, "If you really loved me you would . . ."
9. He expresses contempt for women, or treats them as sex objects.

10. He abuses drugs or alcohol and pressures you to take them with him even when you don't want to.
11. He blames you when he or others mistreat you and say that you provoked it.
12. He has a history of bad relationships and blames other people for his problems.
13. His statements or actions indicate that he thinks men should be in control and that women should do as they're told.
14. He has hit, pushed, choked, restrained, kicked, or physically hurt you.
15. Your family and friends have warned you about him or told you they were worried for your safety.

All too often, the abuser will blame the victim for the abuse. The guilt placed on the victim is a tremendous burden and is the primary cause for low self-esteem in victims. Perpetrators are always responsible for their actions. The abuse is not the fault of the victim.

People stay in abusive relationships for many reasons, but they don't stay because it really isn't that bad. Any abuse is bad abuse. There is no such thing as good abuse or justifiable abuse. Know the signs to watch for, and know how to prevent abuse. Again, prevention of this type of sexual assault will require a great deal of education.

Teen Dating Violence Prevention for Parents

Teach your teenager to protect herself. Help your teen—regardless of gender—become aware of the issues involved in teen dating violence. Encourage your teen to evaluate the safety of various situations. Brainstorm all possible ways of handling a situation, using events from the newspaper, experience of a friend, television, or movies. Help teens establish and develop self-awareness by encouraging them to think, choose, and make decisions for themselves.

Teach your teenager to be assertive. Assertiveness is the ability to exercise one's own rights while respecting the rights of others. It means communicating exactly what you want and don't want, standing up for yourself, and stating your opinions, thoughts, and feelings. Help your teen learn the difference between passive, assertive, and aggressive behavior. A self-defense course can develop assertiveness skills. Ask your teen, "Have you ever said, 'yes,' when you wanted to say, 'no'?" Practice what the teen could say or do if given another chance.

Help your teenager understand what a healthy relationship is. Point out features of healthy relationships from books, movies, or real life. In addition to feelings of love, emphasize the following characteristics of healthy relationships:

- Both partners give and take, each getting their way some of the time and compromising some of the time.
- Partners respect each other and value each other's opinion.
- They support and encourage each other in their individual goals and ambitions.
- They trust each other. Jealousy is not healthy and is not part of a healthy relationship.
- Neither one is afraid of the other person.
- They communicate openly and honestly, and make their partners feel safe in expressing their opinion, even when it differs with the other partner.
- They share responsibility in decision-making.
- They accept the differences between them and don't try to control the relationship.
- They encourage each other to have friends and activities outside the relationship.
- Each partner tries their best to be supportive, caring, and respectful of the other person's wishes.

Domestic Violence

There is a slight difference between domestic violence and violence that takes place in a dating relationship. However, an adult victim of domestic violence may have had several dating relationships that were violent prior to her present violent relationship. This factor may have caused her to have less self-esteem and it also may have conditioned her to believe that all normal relationships are violent and abusive. She may feel less hopeful, more isolated, and more adept at covering up the abuse and making excuses for her abusive partner.

Each year, millions of women are abused by their partners. Very few victims will tell anyone, including friends, relatives, neighbors, or the police. Victims of domestic violence come from all cultures, income groups, ages, and religions. They share common feelings of helplessness, isolation, guilt, fear, and shame. When a woman feels trapped in a violent relationship, often the greatest hurdle that she can overcome is denial. At some point, she first will have to accept the situation as it is, without sugarcoating it or pretending that it isn't a problem. She also will have to come to the reality that her partner's promises to change and never abuse her again are false.

She may not have anyone who can help her come to this conclusion, and if she hasn't sought support, it will be her own decision. Many times, battered women will put up with the abuse as long as their children are not threatened. Once the children are in danger, the mother's protective nature toward their children gives her enormous courage and they will finally leave.

Steps to Freedom

Don't ignore the problem, or make excuses to yourself about his behavior.

Talk to someone. Part of the abuser's power comes from secrecy. Victims often are ashamed to let anyone know about intimate family problems.

Go to a friend or neighbor, or call a domestic violence hotline.

Plan ahead and know what you will do if you are attacked again.

If you decide to leave, choose a safe place to go.

Set aside some money.

Put important papers—marriage license, birth certificates, and check-books—in a place where you can get them quickly.

Learn to think independently.

Try to plan for the future and set goals for yourself.

All of the above steps should be done discreetly, without the abuser's knowledge. Do not let him know you are thinking about leaving or getting help.

Be careful not to leave domestic violence literature around the house where he may find it. If he finds out what your plans are, he may close your bank account, restrict your access outside the house, or even hold your children hostage so that you don't leave him.

If You Are Hurt, What Can You Do?

There are no easy answers, but there are things you can do to protect yourself. As with a stalker, a person who commits continual domestic violence gets more dangerous as the possibility of losing his "property" looms closer and closer. You should realize that this kind of criminal might not honor any restraining order or verbal warning from the police or a judge. You may have to get a weapon and learn to use it to protect yourself. I rarely recommend lethal weapons for most potential victims, but in this case, it may come down to either you physically stopping him or him killing you and your family. Make sure to follow all of these steps first:

- Call the police or sheriff. Assault, even by family members, is a crime. The police often have information about shelters and other agencies that help victims of domestic violence.
- Leave, or have someone come and stay with you.
- Go to a battered women's shelter—call a crisis hotline in your community or a health center to locate a shelter. If you believe that you, or your children, are in danger, leave immediately.
- Get medical attention from your doctor or a hospital emergency

room. Ask the staff to photograph your injuries and keep detailed records in case you decide to take legal action.

• Contact your family court for information about a civil protection order that does not involve criminal charges or penalties.

....

Reality Check:
There are no guarantees. There are risks to leaving as well as staying.

....

Many people don't understand why women stay with abusive men. There are many factors as to why people stay in abusive relationships; from economic dependency to children, lack of realistic options, and lack of self-esteem. Whatever the reason for staying, there is one important reason to leave—you do not deserve to be abused and mistreated.

If you stay, the abuse almost certainly will get worse. The violence will escalate. If you leave, you also may enrage the abuser, and he may become more violent if he can get to you. This is why you definitely will need all the professional help you can get—therapists, domestic violence shelters, counselors, law enforcement authorities—to help you escape. I urge you to take action and contact the appropriate domestic violence contact numbers in the "Resources" section of this book. You are not alone. There are many other women who have been in your situation who can assist you in making the right decision for you and your family.

What Men Must Know

Chapter Sixteen

Advice for Men

I t is time for men to change, time for us to halt rape, sexual harassment, stalking, and domestic violence. Men can no longer keep silent while others continue their rampage. Men absolutely have to change the way they live and interact with others. If you're a man or boy reading this chapter, you must consider that if you do nothing to stop the violence, then you are part of the problem. Take a look at these figures and consider your responsibility to do something to change yourself and other men:

- One in five college women survives rape or attempted rape.
- 84 percent of survivors know their attacker.
- 57 percent of rapes happen on dates.
- 92 percent of the time, a woman reporting a rape is telling the truth.
- 75 percent of men and 55 percent of women involved in acquaintance rape are drinking or taking drugs just before the attack.
- One in twelve men admits to committing acts that meet the legal definition of rape or attempted rape.
- 42 percent of rape survivors tell no one about the rape.
- 84 percent of rape survivors try unsuccessfully to reason with the rapist.

Although this book is primarily for women, I could not write a book about acquaintance rape without saying something to men as well. We live in a highly sexualized society, and women have not yet achieved full equality. It seems to me almost impossible to grow up as a male in this society and not to think about or fantasize about the act of rape. Does having such thoughts make someone a rapist? No. We all have thoughts and fantasies of a sexual nature that we wouldn't want made public.

In the course of my work to eliminate rape in our society, I have presented crime prevention seminars to hundreds of thousands of people. I have run into a series of common responses from a man's perspective. Men's questions and responses center on two main issues:

1. Their concerns about women who lead them on, flirt heavily with them, and then, when the man has reached his sexual peak, say "no" to sexual intercourse.

2. Their concern that women may be claiming to have been raped in order to get even with a man or to hurt him and ruin his reputation.

The first statement implies that a man is not really responsible for his actions beyond a certain point and that, if a woman wants to avoid getting raped, she shouldn't turn a man on to such a degree that he can't stop himself. In questioning men about their ability to control their sexual arousal, I asked them if there had been any occasion in their lives when they suddenly had to stop during intercourse. In one case, a young man had been fondling his girlfriend when her mother came home unexpectedly, surprising him in the act. What was interesting about this situation is that the girl had tried to get him to stop repeatedly without success. He said, "I'm too turned on to stop now," but when her mother walked in on them, he somehow found the self-control to stop immediately. In fact, he said his erection was gone almost at once.

· ·

Reality Check:
There is no point at which a man cannot control himself during sexual arousal. He may not want to control himself, but he can stop.

· ·

Let's make this a bit more personal and take it a step farther. Suppose you (a man) were out of work, had no money, hadn't worked for a long time, and money was all you could think about. You dreamed about it every night. Your creditors were banging on your door and harassing you on a daily basis. You had to have some money. So you went to a bank and, asked for a loan, which the bank refused. You then went up to the teller's window and watched her count the money on the other side of the counter. When you felt as if you couldn't take it anymore, you grabbed a handful of bills from the teller and ran out of the bank.

Did you commit a crime? Would the bank prosecute you? Would you expect to go to jail if caught? I hope you would answer yes, because you did indeed break the law and the consequences for your actions are that you will go to a state prison for a number of years. Do you see the analogy? If we use the example of robbing a bank, then perhaps you can see that, even though you needed the money and were in debt, you still committed a crime! Even though you felt the bank tempted you with all that money lying around, you still took what did not belong to you and committed a felony. Can you logically say that the bank caused you to commit robbery, because it was enticing you with its financial reserves? The tellers even had the audacity to count the money in the open. Likewise, you could say that if they didn't want to get robbed, then they shouldn't have been so provocative with their money.

In the same manner, when you are physically turned on, that does not give you the right to take what doesn't belong to you. You may feel that your date shouldn't be a tease and turn you on, or that she should not drink and get you worked up so that you do not want to stop. If you don't like the way you are being treated, and if you feel as if she is manipulating you, then get up and leave. You are in control. You always have a choice. It doesn't matter what you think at this point. We have all had fantasies of robbing a bank and getting away with it. No one will put you in jail for robbing a bank in your mind, but the minute you decide to act out your fantasy, you have committed a crime and can go to jail. It's the same in a rape situation. The minute you take action and force sex with someone against her will, or without her conscious consent, you have committed the crime of rape and can go to jail.

Beyond getting caught and what happens to you, think about the woman. The minute you physically commit rape, you have abused a woman and possibly scarred her for the rest of her life.

Following are some of the common misperceptions, misunderstandings, and myths that many men harbor:

Myth: If she didn't struggle, it wasn't rape.

Fact: Rape is sex without consent, whether there is a struggle or not.

Myth: If she goes along with it, it isn't rape.

Fact: Rape is rape if she feels she has no choice or is incoherent or unconscious.

Myth: If she didn't scream, it wasn't rape.

Fact: The greatest fear in a rape victim is the fear of being killed. She may not scream because she is too frightened.

Myth: If she had sex before, or has sex frequently, it wasn't rape or she deserved it.

Fact: Her sexual history and yours, even if it involves her, has nothing to do with this situation. Prior consent is not current consent.

Myth: Women are to blame for rape if they are in "risky situations."

Fact: A woman is no more to blame for being raped because she was in a risky situation, than a deer is for wandering into the sights of the hunter. Remember, the criminal is at fault, not the victim!

Myth: Women who wear provocative clothes should expect to be raped.

Fact: What she wears has nothing to do with the behavior of the rapist. To provoke someone is to incite or cause to happen. Some women wear attention-getting clothes to attract attention, but that must not be taken as an invitation to rape. If a man wears tight jeans that attract attention to his crotch, does that mean he wants to be raped? Of course not! Rape is about power, not about sex. Babies and senior citizens also get raped. We don't question the suggestiveness of baby attire or an old person's clothing. Doing so is just another method of shifting the blame from the criminal to the victim.

Criminals start lives of crime in their thoughts before their actions get them into trouble with the law. You are or will become what you consistently think about. As men, we must all take responsibility for our own thoughts and actions.

Reality Check:
No one turns you on. You turn yourself on with
the thoughts that are going on inside your head.

The thoughts are yours, not hers. You have control over them; she doesn't. You can change your thoughts. You can continue to think about her, about how you want to "make it with her," and get yourself all worked up so that your conscience cannot reach you anymore. Realize that only you turn yourself on, and only you turn yourself off.

It's time to stop blaming women and others for men's actions. Men are in control. Men do the deed. Men break the law. It is men who have the problem with violence. You may be thinking, "What about women? Don't women rape? Don't women stalk? Don't women sexually harass? Don't women commit domestic violence?" Yes. But the figures indicate that men, not women, commit the vast majority of crimes of violence. So, it's men who have the problem, and it's up to us to stop it.

After She Says No, It's Rape!

If you have sex with someone who cannot give consent due to being incapacitated by alcohol or drugs or is otherwise unconscious, you have committed rape!

If you have sex with someone and get her unwilling consent or lack of resistance due to your verbal, physical, or emotional threats, then you have made it impossible for her to say, "no," therefore you have committed rape.

Can she change her mind? Yes. If she originally wanted to have sex, and at the last minute decides she no longer wants to go through with it, it is her right to say, "no," and to stop it, just as stopping at the last minute is your right. A man has the same right to "pull out" in the middle of intercourse, regardless of whether a woman wants to continue or not. So a woman has the right to stop, regardless of your desires and wants at the moment.

You break the law when you persist in your sexual advances after she has said, "no." It is also rape if she is incapacitated so that her ability to say, "no," is impaired.

Many men fear the possibility that a woman may be manipulating them into a sexual situation only to change her mind on a whim. Is this a real problem? Sometimes, women do manipulate men to get what they want from them. Of course men do the same thing. If you feel that a woman is teasing you and playing with your emotions, rather than risk a potential rape situation with her, sit down and talk to her. Tell her exactly what you feel and that you're confused by her inconsistent behavior.

You might say:

"Look, I don't appreciate the way I'm being treated."

"I'm getting a lot of mixed messages from you. It seems one minute you want to have sex and the next minute you don't. What's going on?"

"I want you to know that this is your decision too, and I'm not going to take advantage of you. Please be honest with me and tell me what you want. Yes or no."

Some men are also concerned that a woman might attempt to ruin a man's reputation by making up a rape story.

Reality Check:

No person in her right mind would fabricate a rape charge and go through all of the terror and trauma of reporting it to the police, taking the evidentiary exam, and exposing herself to the aftermath of insinuations and abuse by friends, family, and the judicial system unless something had occurred.

Some men also are concerned that a woman might attempt to ruin a man's reputation by making up a rape story.

It's hard for some men to grasp what a woman goes through at the time of the rape, with the ongoing trauma that can last for years, unless he has himself been raped or been touched by the rape of a sister or close friend.

For some men, thinking about rape can be a pleasant sexual fantasy. To them, rape is being ravished by several women and satiated until they're exhausted. The pain that in reality goes along with an actual rape is generally missing from the male fantasy. Women rarely rape men. Some do, but the real threat for men is not being raped by women, but by other men. If you remember that rape is an act of aggression and power, not sex, then maybe you can see yourself as a potential victim.

Imagine yourself going out with a bunch of guys. Maybe you all go to a football game. You have a great time and afterward you all go to a local bar for more than a few drinks. On the way home, something happens and these guys who you thought were your friends suddenly turn on you and attack. They take you to a vacant lot, beat you up, and decide to rape you. You fight like hell, but you're outnumbered. They hold you down and brutally rape you for four or five hours. They punch you and kick you, all the while telling you how much you're enjoying it. Then it's over. They tell you that if you ever tell anyone, they'll come back and kill you. After they leave you lying on the ground, hurt and bleeding, you finally get up and make your way to a gas station where you try to tell the attendants about what happened. They laugh and call you a drunk and other epithets. Then they tell you to get lost. You finally get to a police station. They are skeptical and ask whether you're a homosexual. You can hear them snickering behind your back. They say, "There's no way I'd let any guy do that to me. I'd kill him first." Another one says, "I'd kill myself first." They keep asking you why you didn't fight back? You try to explain that there were four of them and that there was no way to stop them. They take the report, but you sense that they won't be doing anything about it.

Telling your girlfriend is a big mistake. She thinks you must have done something to provoke the incident. Then she starts wondering about your sexuality, or whether you've cheated on her. You can feel her getting colder toward you, and you think that maybe she thinks that this was all your fault.

Now you know you can never tell your parents. Your mom might understand, but there's no way your father could ever handle it.

Your pain does not end there. You have difficulty sleeping at night, and the guys who raped you call you from time to time to threaten you should you decide to tell anyone. The fear and anxiety are keeping you as a prisoner in your own apartment. You decide to drop the case and tell the police you don't want to prosecute. You know that because you all had several drinks together, everyone would think you invited the attack. You feel like you are all alone.

No one understands the pain and humiliation that you are going through, and for the first time in your life, you contemplate suicide. If only someone would believe you!

Then one day a woman comes up to you and tells you she is from the women's support group on campus. She says she would like to talk to you. You're reluctant, but she confides that like you, she too was a victim of rape. She puts you in touch with the rape crisis center counselor. After a while you join a support group of other rape victims, some of whom are men, and, for the first time since the assault, you know you are not alone, that you are not the only victim of rape. Now the long healing process begins.

Does this sound impossible? Although it was a gang rape, the aftermath, where the victim can't get support from those to whom she turns for help, is actually a very common date/acquaintance rape scenario.

Rape, date/acquaintance rape, sexual assault, stalking, sexual harassment, and domestic violence are all crimes of power. The primary reason for the abuse is to gain power. This power is taken from another person through deception, intimidation, and physical force.

* * *

Reality Check:
Remember that rape is a crime of power, not sex, so whether you're a male or female, it can happen to you.

* * *

In reality most abusers have very low self-esteem. Their lives are out of control, and they feel powerless to change things. Instead of looking within to find an inner sense of personal power, which is the only kind that lasts, they look outside themselves, mistakenly feeling that the only way to get power is from another person. This belief is not valid and will not make you feel more powerful.

So why don't rapists try to steal power from other men? That is so because rapists are generally cowardly individuals who feel inferior to other men. They can steal power only from someone they see as being "less" than they are. They will attack a woman, young girl, or older female, i.e., one who appears vulnerable, weak, and alone. That's why women who have great personal power and confidence are not as likely to be attacked. These women present themselves as more formidable adversaries. In the field of crime prevention, we would say they are hardened targets instead of soft targets.

Preventing rape is, in reality, the responsibility of all men. But rape is not just an act of violence that occurs out of nowhere; it has its causes and sources. As in all physical behavior, rape starts in the mind. In order to change the behavior, we must change the thoughts that create it.

Over the centuries women have become objects; objects to be wanted, desired, taken, and used. Anything that objectifies women creates and maintains a society that supports rape ideas.

Some Advice for Men

Know your sexual desires and limits. Communicate them clearly.

Be aware of social pressures.

It's okay not to "score."

Being turned down when you ask for sex is not in any way a rejection of you personally.

Women who say "no" to sex are not rejecting you; they are expressing their desire not to participate in a single act.

Your desires may be beyond your control, but your actions are well within your control.

Accept the woman's decision. "No" means "no."

Don't read other meanings into the answer . . . even based on past experience with this or other women.

Don't continue after "no." If you're thinking the woman doesn't mean it, simply stop and ask. Then respect her decision.

Don't assume that just because a woman dresses in a sexy manner and flirts, she wants to have sexual intercourse.

Don't assume that previous permission for sexual contact applies to the current situation.

Avoid excessive use of alcohol and/or drugs.

There is an epidemic of violence in relationships, and it's all about control. Relationships run by control and/or violence are unhealthy and harmful to both individuals, and they will never be as rewarding as healthy, loving relationships.

Men can change their attitudes and behavior and can see that treating women respectfully and equitably has great benefits for men as well. I have had a conversation with a man who has begun to realize that he may have forced himself on a nonconsenting woman at one time or another. If it occurs to you as you are reading this book that you have hurt someone in this way, you can get help and break the cycle. I encourage you to do so, as your life will be transformed for the better in the process. Here is how to begin:

- Realize that your behavior is covering up insecurity and that you damage your family, your relationships, and yourself when you act in a violent manner.
- Be aware that you break the law when you physically hurt someone.
- Take responsibility for your actions and get help.
- When you feel tension building, get away.
- Work off angry energy through a walk, a project, or a sport.
- Call a domestic violence hotline or health center and ask about counseling and support groups.

Breaking Up

A time of great vulnerability is when a relationship is coming to an end. Most dating and domestic violence occur when the relationship is breaking up. The breaking up experience can be very difficult for both parties. Below is a list of "do's" and " don'ts" that may help make breaking up easier to get through.

DO

Explain your reasons for breaking up if you can

Be respectful and listen

Find ways to take care of your feelings: Keep a journal, talk to friends, exercise, play sports, listen to music, allow yourself to cry

Seek counseling

DON'T

Threaten

Have sex one last time

Follow the other person to see whether he or she is going out with someone

Call unless you've both agreed this is okay

Break up to scare the person into doing things your way

Get even

Try to get pregnant or cause a pregnancy

Call names, spread rumors, or otherwise try to get revenge

Isolate yourself or be alone

Assume being friends means you will get back together

Love

There are certain images and words describing what love is that lead to confusion and sometimes to bad situations. In fact, some of these messages are actually what love isn't. There are many things about love that can't be summed up in a word. Here are two lists to help you sort out what love is or isn't. These lists are to help you decide how you want to be treated.

LOVE IS...	LOVE ISN'T...
Responsibility	Jealousy
Hard work	Possessiveness
Pleasure	Pain
Commitment	Violence
Caring	Obsession
Honesty	Being selfish
Trust	Cruelty
Communication	Getting pregnant
Sharing	Making someone pregnant
Compromising	Dependency
Closeness	Giving up who you are
Recognizing differences	Intimidation
Vulnerability	Scoring
Openness	Fear
Respect	Proving yourself
Friendship	Manipulation
Strong positive feelings	Expecting all your needs to be met by the other person

Conflict

Some men find it extremely difficult to deal with conflict. Conflict is part of everyday life. You can't always avoid conflict, but you can learn to manage it without violence. Following are some of the skills that you need to manage personal conflict.

Understand your own feelings about conflict. This means recognizing your "triggers," words or actions that immediately provoke an emotional response such as anger. It could be a facial expression, a tone of voice, a pointing finger, a certain phrase. Once you know your triggers, you can better control your emotions.

Practice active listening. Go beyond hearing just words—try to understand what the other person is really saying. Listen carefully instead of thinking about what you're going to say next. Active listening requires concentration and body language that says you are paying attention and care about what the other person has to say.

Generate options for resolving a conflict. Many people can think of only two ways to manage conflict—fighting or avoiding the problem. Get the facts straight, brainstorm all ideas that might help resolve the argument, and discuss the pros, cons, and consequences of continuing such a disagreement. If you're left with raging emotions that lead to more problems, then your style isn't working. Try to learn new conflict resolution techniques. There are many personal growth programs that can give you a toolbox for communicating better and avoiding confrontation. Call your local community college, or talk to friends or religious leaders who can refer you to someone who can help.

State your needs and define the problem. Talk about the issues without insulting or blaming the other person. Don't state your position; that's simply your solution to the problem. Before you can resolve a problem, you have to agree about what the problem is. Get to the root of the conflict before you start looking for a solution. Take a look at what is said and what is really needed.

Together discuss various ways of meeting needs or solving the problem. Be flexible and open-minded. Decide who will be responsible for a specific action after reaching agreement on a plan.

Tips for Making Peace

Choose a convenient time to have a discussion.

Plan ahead.

Talk directly.

Don't blame or name-call.

Give information.

Listen.

Show that you are listening.

Talk through the issues.

Work on a solution.

Follow through.

If you can't work it out, get help.

There is no excuse for not getting help. There are hundreds of rape- and violence-prevention centers around the United States and Canada that are geared to help men prevent violence against women. There is a partial list of centers in the "Resources" section of this book that can help you whether you are a batterer, a survivor of battering, or have a problem with forced sexual contact. Getting help does not make you less of a man. It means you have the courage to know when an objective viewpoint is needed.

I urge you to have the courage to be part of the solution by standing up for nonviolence, and not to be part of the problem by remaining silent.

Chapter Seventeen

Nonviolent Communication

Changing the Way We Speak, a Search for Compassion

During my years as a crime prevention speaker, I realized that there was a great need for a deeper analysis of the way we think and speak. I saw that men and women wanted more than to just have me tell them what not to do; they wanted a real solution to their communication problems.

All of the preceding chapters have dealt with rape prevention in the most straightforward manner. The purpose of those chapters is to stop the violence. The purpose of this chapter is to help men and women find a new way to communicate in a more compassionate manner that will stop the violence before it ever becomes physical.

Most of us don't think of our everyday communication as being violent, but every thought and word we say contributes either to harmony or to violence in our actions. When we think of violence, we tend to think only of physical violence, but there is a deeper kind of violence that permeates our relationships, and that is emotional violence. This is the kind of turbulence that many of us live in most of the time. We build our relationships in a kind of storm where our words and thoughts constantly cut and slash those we care about. Sometimes we hurt others consciously, but most of the time, we do it unconsciously, because that's the only way we know how to communicate. We say things without thinking. We attack and defend ourselves on a daily basis. These are not the words of thinking, conscious, compassionate people, but of unconscious, unthinking, and unloving people. From our earliest years, we've learned these hurtful words from family, friends, and associates. We create relationships like our parents and grandparents, not because we want to, but because this is all we know. It's time to learn a new way of communicating.

We don't just speak and hear words, we attach meanings to them based on our own history, agendas, and feelings. Harmless words that are said in an offhand manner can open up wounds that have never healed since childhood. Because our language is often fuzzy and subjective, there is a need for a different language.

Two years ago I became aware of a unique new approach to communication. It was developed by Marshall B. Rosenberg, Ph. D., in his book: *Nonviolent Communication, A Language of Life*. Not only is this remarkable book's approach transforming the way we in this country look at language, but it has also been instrumental in transforming the way people speak in countries all over the world.

What's wrong with our communication?

If you want to know what's wrong, all you have to do is listen. Listen to the media, your family, friends, coworkers, and classmates. What do you hear? If you're like me, you hear judgment, anger, name-calling, criticism, and fear. What you don't hear most of the time is compassionate language.

We live in a time when civil discourse seems to be extinct. Most of us know that one of the most common reasons why relationships fail is poor communication. If we all know how to communicate, then why do our words contaminate our relationships and drive us farther apart?

What blocks our ability to communicate with compassion?

Judgments

In his book, Rosenberg identifies the things that block compassion. One block is moralistic judgments. In my seminars at colleges around the country, I have heard over and over again, generalizations, such as: "All women are _____." or, "all men are _____." You fill in the blanks. These kinds of vast generalizations come from our tendency to make judgments based on our beliefs.

We must find a way to separate what others say and do from our judgments of them. The only way to really change the toxic environment of our relationships is to remove the judgments. I'm not talking about making a judgment about what is the best thing to do in your life. I'm talking about judging other people's decisions as right or wrong. That is called a "moralistic judgment." As long as you think in these terms, that the other person is right or wrong, you are sitting in judgment. You can't communicate compassion and understanding if you are in judgment. Think about the ways you judge others. Whenever you have judged someone, has it brought the two of you closer together, or has it driven you apart? Understand that I'm not talking about rape here, but about the everyday right and wrong labeling that we do to others.

Comparisons

Making comparisons is another way of alienating ourselves from others. If I compare myself to other men, I will probably believe that I am inadequate. If a woman compares herself to other women, she too will probably put herself down for not measuring up. Using comparisons separates us from others because the other person usually feels that she or he is not measuring up and has been attacked. A person who feels attacked will respond either by withdrawing or by defending herself or himself, or by attacking in return.

Denial of responsibility

We have talked a great deal in this book about denying responsibility when it comes to relationships. Each of us is responsible for our own thoughts, feelings, and actions, but we are not responsible for what someone else thinks, feels, or does. First, we have to identify what we think, how we feel, and why we act the way we do. Many of us obscure our responsibility by pretending that we have no choice in the matter. We act like puppets who have no control over our own lives, and we blame every act on something else or someone else.

Before we can change our language, we have to change the way we think. Our words come from our thoughts. Before you automatically say something that will hurt the other person, take a moment and think about what you want to communicate. Will it bring the two of you closer together or drive you apart? We have to become responsible for our every word, because our words define us. Taking responsibility for our language will require intense focus because so much of our speech patterns are about denying responsibility. Here are some ways in which our language affirms our lack of being responsible.

Vague forces

Have you ever heard yourself say, "I just had to do that"? This kind of statement is often made without thinking. It refers to some vague impersonal force that makes us do things. We often say this as an excuse to tell people that we had no choice. Our first step to total responsibility is to know that we have made a choice here to blame our actions on something outside our control. Of course, this vague force doesn't exist.

Gender blame

Another way I get out of being totally responsible is by blaming my actions on the fact that I am a man or a woman. In this way I am telling people that my gender controls my words and actions. Of course, nothing could be further from the truth. Men and women are not bound by their gender to act in any particular fashion, unless that is their choice. Men don't have to behave like other men, and women don't have to behave like other women. You can be different if you choose.

Group pressure

Perhaps you think that others are responsible for what you say and do. This is a very common excuse among gang rapists. They will often say that they had no choice because they couldn't go against the group. When we sacrifice our own identity to that of the group, then we have made a choice to follow, instead of to lead. Remember that you always have a choice; however, leadership takes courage.

The actions of others

How many times have you heard yourself say, "You made me do this. You make me happy." When we say this, we misunderstand the fact that although someone's actions may trigger a response in us, that action did not cause the response. We caused it ourselves with our thoughts. Have you ever found yourself overreacting to someone's words or actions? When you look at your response objectively, you'll see that your actions did not fit the trigger. That is because you reacted to a deep emotional wound that has never healed. Once you face that wound and heal it, the trigger will disappear. This kind of situation is very prevalent in parent-child relationships.

The dictates of authority

All of us have felt powerless in a work or school situation. We may have said, "I have to get this work done, or I'll fail the course." If you're in a work situation, you might say; "I have to endure this sexual harassment because I'm afraid that if I report it, I'll lose my job." In both cases, you can either change or change the situation. Of course, no matter which choice you make, it brings freedom because you are not content to remain a victim. If you are unwilling to change the way you look at sexual harassment on the job, and you are also unwilling to endure it, then you have a choice to either report the behavior or leave the situation. Embrace the fact that you have power in what you thought was a powerless situation. The power comes from your ability to change and control your life. A predator relies on his victim's belief that she is powerless.

Uncontrollable impulses

As this book has illustrated, this has been a time-honored excuse that men deny responsibility for their own sexual behavior. No matter how much we progress, we still hear this excuse that the man couldn't stop. This tired excuse is more pathetic today than ever. There is no reason why men can't control their impulses, unless they choose not to. Women too have used this excuse to justify denying their own power to make healthy choices, whether those choices are food, alcohol, or men. Once you open the door to taking responsibility for your life, you can't, in good conscience, close it again.

If you change the way you look at the work you need to do to pass the course, and you see it as a choice that you've made to further your education and improve your life, instead of as a burden, then you can see the work differently.

The ultimate reality in all relationships is that, if we are conscious, we always have choices. That's why compassionate communication is a conscious choice to think, see, hear, and act differently.

NVC: Rosenberg's Five Steps to Compassionate Language

There are five steps to Nonviolent Communication. Changing the way we communicate takes a great deal of focus and persistence. This process is very simple, but it is not easy. However, I have found that if you will work with these steps, you will drastically change all of your relationships for the better.

Step One: Observing without Evaluating

Look around right now. Stop reading and look around your environment. Try to see it without putting any evaluation on it. If you are upset with someone in a relationship, such as a roommate, coworker, or family member, ask yourself what happened that made you upset? What did the person do? Be careful not to judge the other person's reason or motive for doing what she or he did. Don't evaluate what you have seen or heard. Just observe what happened and stop there. I know it's hard, but in order to take the pain out of our relationships, we must first separate what happened from why it happened.

This is not easy. We have become very used to judging everyone and everything around us without thinking. It is important that you suspend all moralistic judgments about the situation. Try to see it objectively, as though it had happened to someone else, with no connection to you.

In relation to dating, I have heard many a man tell me that if a woman smiled at him, then it meant she wanted more attention. He may have thought that she wanted him to get close to her, to touch her, or even that she wanted to have sex with him. I know this sounds crazy, but it's true. However, if he observes that smile and doesn't attach any meaning to it, then he has no reason to believe that it's a come-on for any further actions on his part. The smile may have something to do with him, or it may not. She may just be thinking a pleasant thought.

Beyond the dating scenario, breaking the link between observation and evaluation will enhance your communication in all relationships. When you start to get conscious of how much you judge, you will begin to see why your relationships suffer.

Judging breaks our compassionate connection with others. Instead of our words building bridges of understanding and love, they become harsh and critical. And what do we all do when we think we're being criticized? We shut down, defend ourselves, or fight back. But no matter what the response, the human connection is destroyed. If this continues, the relationship will eventually disintegrate.

The other part of Step One is to separate your observation from yourself. So often a woman who has been assaulted will judge and condemn herself, even if others don't, for everything she did or didn't do before and after the assault. So here again, if she can separate her actions and words from any evaluations or judgments of them, she will be less likely to blame herself for what happened to her. All of us are so practiced in self-judgment and condemnation that we are quick to blame ourselves for every thing we do that doesn't go the way we want. Is it any wonder our self-esteem is so low?

The question becomes, how do I know whether I'm making an evaluation or not? One way to get conscious of your language is to look for the words *always*, *never*, *ever*, *whenever*, *seldom*, or *frequently*. When these words are used, it is generally a clue that we are making an exaggeration of someone's behavior. This is judgment, and it usually causes the other person to defend himself or herself and to deny the exaggeration.

The Indian Philosopher J. Krishnamurti said, "Observation without evaluation is the highest form of human intelligence."

Step Two: Identifying and Expressing Feelings

In Step One, we talked about separating our evaluations from our observations. Now it is important to understand how we are feeling. Let's go back to our illustration of a woman smiling at a man. We have the observation—she smiled. We've separated the evaluation from her smile. Now it is important to identify what the man is feeling when she smiles. He may think the following thoughts; "I feel like she wants to get to know me. I feel that she likes me. I feel as if she wants me to get closer, or hold her hand, or even that she wants me to come on to her." These statements are not feelings, but thoughts.

When you follow the word *feel* with the expression *like* or *that* or *as if*, you are in a thought, not a feeling. In identifying feelings, it's important to understand the difference between feelings and thoughts. Our everyday language is so automatic that we often say, "I feel" in the middle of a thought, without the slightest inkling that what we're talking about has nothing to do with our feelings.

We often use words such as *feel* without really expressing our feelings. In my illustration of a woman smiling at a man, if he can identify his feelings, then he might think, "I feel good. I feel warm. I feel love." Do you see the difference? His feelings are separate from her actions. He takes ownership and complete responsibility for what he is feeling, but he has not connected what he feels with her smile. Her smile and his feelings are two different events. The smile may be a trigger, which brings up the thought, which causes him to feel something, but the smile did not cause the feeling. His thoughts caused his feelings.

Whenever you react to someone's behavior with a feeling, it's vital to remember that you have a choice as to how you react, and therefore feel, about what you've experienced. If someone does something that irritates you, realize that the irritation is a feeling, based on a thought that you have a choice over. You always have a choice of what you think.

For some of us men, it can be difficult to identify what we're feeling. Boys are generally discouraged from showing feelings. For centuries boys have been taught to keep everything inside and, as the British say, "keep a stiff upper lip," which really means, "don't cry." This inability to show feelings and share with others can be devastating. When their wives leave them, many men find it very difficult to live high-quality lives because their one source of feelings and emotions is gone, and they don't know how to replace it.

Rosenberg, in his book, has an entire list of feelings that will help men identify what's going on inside of them.

Sometimes, we express our feelings in a way that says that others don't approve of us. When we say, "I feel misunderstood, unimportant, or ignored," this indicates that others have control over us, and about the way we feel about ourselves.

For most women, identifying and expressing feelings will come much easier. Girls are allowed to cry if they are sad, and to reach out to others if they need to share their feelings. This makes for a much healthier person. That's one of the reasons why women survive longer when relationships end.

Handling put-downs

In so much of today's communication, we hear people being put down or "dissed" (short for disrespected). Remember the old childhood rhyme? Sticks and stones will break my bones, but words will never hurt me. We now know that one of the great reasons for low self-esteem and broken spirits in our children is the result of hurtful language. That's why Rosenberg identifies it as violent, because these words do more damage than all the broken bones in childhood.

When hurtful language is thrown at us, how do we handle it? For most of us, we
• Blame ourselves and take the remark personally
• Blame others for the situation
• Feel attacked, but do nothing
• Aggressively defend ourselves
• Attack our attacker with even more hurtful language

None of these options increases our connection with the other person, or enhances our relationship.

Rosenberg states that we actually have two more choices here:
• Be aware of your own feelings at the moment and identify your needs.
• Be aware of the feelings and needs of the other person.

Let's go back to our dating scenario where the man sees the woman smiling. He interprets her smile as a come-on, then proceeds to get closer to her and hold her hand and puts his arm around her. She tells him that she's not comfortable with that.

He has a choice as to how he's going to handle this. He can either be offended and withdraw into a shell, or he can defend his actions or say something hurtful, such as she led him on, or she's stuck up and thinks she's too good for him.

At this point she observes that all the warmth and kindness that was so attractive in him earlier in the evening is gone.

Now she too feels hurt. They both had other choices, but they reacted unconsciously to the situation. They handled this situation as they've probably handled hundreds of other situations like it . . . without thinking.

If she is conscious of her language and feelings, she will know that she can choose to respond differently. She may feel that deep down she likes him and doesn't want to hurt him or end the relationship.

However, if she identifies her own feelings and her own needs and accepts them, then she can talk to him on a level that doesn't cause him to defend himself or feel attacked. She might tell him that when he said that she had led him on, and that she was too stuck up, she felt sad. She could also tell him that she needs to feel comfortable and safe before she gets too close to him. At this point he has a choice. If he's conscious, and not so deep in his hurt feelings that he can't be reached, then he can hear that she is not attacking him and that she has made a request for patience. He might also sense that she feels vulnerable and needs to feel safe before proceeding with intimacy.

Step Three: Identifying Your Needs

Now that you know what you feel, the next step is to figure out what you need from the situation. In every situation involving relationships, whether they are personal or professional, we all have needs. The stress and dysfunction comes when we can't get our needs met. We have discussed observing the situation without evaluation. We have also talked about identifying our feelings. Remember that our feelings come from our thoughts, which are often triggered by our past experiences. Next we must address what need inside of us is not getting met.

In our dating situation, the woman's need might be to be respected and listened to. She may have had a long history of doing things for others and not for herself. Perhaps her needs are buried very deep inside of her. She may not know what she is really looking for in a relationship. His need may be to be important to her. He may want friendship, love, support, and companionship. Both of them want to be important to the other person. Both of them want to be listened to and be respected. And both want to be loved.

Their next step is to be aware of each other's feelings and needs. She might ask him whether he felt rejected when she pulled back from his touch. She can also ask him whether he needs to feel attractive to her. What she's really trying to do here is to get him to share his feelings. By asking him to share his feelings, she has attempted to lift the relationship to a whole new level, one in which both can get their needs met.

Successful relationships are based on people communicating their feelings and needs to one another in a nonjudgmental manner. I know that many times I have heard men tell me that the women in their lives expect them to know their needs.

I remember an old TV program called *The Dick Van Dyke Show*. It was a popular TV show in the 1960s. One of the funniest moments occurred when Laura (Mary Tyler Moore) would start to cry. Rob, her husband (Dick Van Dyke), would ask her what was the matter? She would sob and wail and say, "If you don't know, I'm certainly not going to tell you."

Yes, that was TV comedy, but it was so true. It is still true. In so many cases, I have heard women vent their frustration about their men, because they think that if they are in a relationship, the man should know what their needs and feelings are.

So often the man is befuddled when a woman explodes in tears and rage, and he has no idea what's going on with her. This kind of explosive situation happens when one person is not getting his or her needs met. The partner may have been unresponsive to the other person's needs, but too often the partner indicates that she or he had no idea that needs were going unmet. If you want your needs to be met, you must acknowledge them to yourself and then communicate them honestly and without judgment to your partner.

Step Four: Making a Request:

So here we are at the last step. Making a request sounds simple, doesn't it? It really is simple, but once again we face the years of conditioning that our families and society have taught us that obscures our communication. Remember to keep your request positive. When you ask someone to not do something, you run the risk of the other person resisting your request because your language is confusing. You also run the risk of their going along with your request, but not meeting your needs.

In our dating scenario, when the woman told the man that she wasn't comfortable with him putting his arm around her, she was actually making a negative request. She was telling him what not to do, but not what to do. He got confused and hurt and withdrew completely. If she had made her request a positive one, i.e., "Instead of putting your arm around me, I would feel more comfortable if we held hands. Is that okay with you?" Now she has given him the message that his putting his arm around her is making her uncomfortable, but she's also told him what kind of intimacy she is comfortable with. He can then respond without feeling as if she's rejected him.

It's also important to make your request specific and easy to understand. This can be challenging for some women because they may have been taught not to voice their needs. Avoid vague, abstract language, as it can be confusing and difficult to understand. What do I mean when I say make your request specific? In our dating example, if after the man had put his arm around the woman, she had said, "I want you to respect me," he would have been confused because he wouldn't have understood the connection between putting his arm around her and her not being respected. He most certainly would have jumped to the conclusion that she was accusing him of trying to take advantage of her. Remember that you may think you are very clear in your request, but the other person may not be hearing what you think you are saying. That's why it is a good idea to ask the other person to tell you what she or he heard you say. You'll be surprised at how many times the message received is different from the message sent.

Requests vs. Demands

For men, the challenge is in making a request rather than a demand. First of all, be sure that you realize that if you are in a position of authority over another person, even when you are making a request, that person may be hearing it as a demand.

If another person hears a demand coming from you, that person will either submit or rebel. The question is then, how do you know whether what you're saying is a request or a demand? The answer lies in your choice of what you do if your request is not complied with. If you make a request, and the person says no, and you criticize, judge, or punish the person for saying no, then you have made a demand, not a request. The purpose of NVC is not to manipulate and control people. The purpose is to find a common ground where both people can get their needs met. The idea here is to transform relationships from win-lose to win-win.

Step Five: Empathy: The Key to Understanding

We have covered observation, evaluation, feelings, needs, and making requests. The other side of making a request is receiving the request with empathy. Empathy is the key to understanding another person's feelings and needs. It is more than just listening; it is listening with your heart. It occurs only when you are really present with that other person. By present, I mean that you are not in your thoughts, analyzing, judging, consoling, or educating the the other person. In short, you are not doing anything that stops that person's sharing of what she or he is feeling.

Once again, this is simple but not easy. We all tend to want to fix others when they tell us their problems. This is especially true with men. I know in my own case, it is very difficult to not give my wife suggestions when she comes to me with a problem. I think it must be in a man's DNA to want to take care of his mate and make sure that he solves all her problems.

Part of the key to listening with empathy is to take yourself beyond the other person's words to try to get a sense of what that person really needs. If someone comes at you with a strong judgment or accusation, the first tendency is to deny or defend or attack. Take a breath and ask what are they feeling?. All criticism, attacks, insults, and judgments will subside when you focus your attention on the feelings and needs behind the words.

How do you know whether the other person has felt your empathy? When the other person feels heard with empathy, that person will feel a sense of relief. Often the person will then stop talking. I remember a counseling session that I had with a Jesuit priest many years ago. After I had unloaded all my problems, I noticed that he said very little during the session. He didn't give me any advice, but he gave me empathy. I could feel his understanding and compassion for me. When I finally stopped sharing, I asked him about the session. He said his only purpose was to be there and let me know that he understood my pain and that I was not alone. That was more important than all the advice that any psychologist or psychiatrist could have given me. After the session was over, I felt relieved that a huge burden had been lifted off my shoulders. That is the power of empathy. This chapter is only a brief introduction to nonviolent communication. I hope it will inspire you to investigate NVC. It is the most powerful communication guide that I have ever seen. If you study it and use it on a daily basis, your relationships will be transformed.

For more information on Marshall Rosenberg's book, *Nonviolent Communication, A Language of Life*, and other materials related to his work, contact

CNVC, Center for Nonviolent Communication:

2428 Foothill Blvd., Suite E

La Crescenta, CA 91214

Ph. 800-255-7696

Or visit their website: www.cnvc.org.

Resources

In a situation of danger or imminent danger, always call 9-1-1 or another emergency number. To begin to assemble the resources to cope after an assault has taken place, below are national crisis hotlines. You can find similar hotlines in your local Yellow Pages, usually listed under "Crisis Intervention." Most larger cities and colleges have rape crisis centers.

Are You In Crisis Right Now?

In danger? – Call 911
In crisis? – Call 1-800-656-HOPE (4673)

This is the National Sexual Assault Hotline, operated by RAINN, 24 hours a day. You can ask them for the number for your local rape crisis center. If you need to speak to a woman, feel free to ask for one. You can also contact your local Rape Crisis Center by dialing (411) information in your area.

Basic Hotlines

Rape Crisis: 1-800-656-HOPE (4673)
Self Injury: 1-800-DON'T-CUT (366-8288)
Suicide Hotline: 1-800-273-TALK, 1-800-SUICIDE (784-2433)
Domestic Violence: 1-800-799-SAFE (7233)
Gay & Lesbian: 1-888-THE-GLNH (843-4564)

American Domestic Crisis Line: 1-866-USWOMEN (1-866-879-6636)

Domestic Violence: 1-800-621-HOPE (1-800-621-4673)

Domestic Violence Crisis Line: 1-800-494-8100

National Child Abuse Hotline/ChildhelpUSA: 1-800-4-A-CHILD

National Domestic Violence Hotline: 1-800-799-SAFE (1-800-799-7223)

National Women's Health Resource Line: 1-800-994-9662

Abuse and Assault: 1-800-962-2873

Citizen Complaint Center, Civil Rights Division: 202-514-4718

Crime Victims' Counseling Services: 718-875-5862

AIDS Prevention: 1-800-322-8911

AIDS HIV: 1-800-342-2437

Ask a Nurse (24 hr. free medical advice: 1-800-535-1111

"How to end domestic violence in your community" kit: 1-800-777-1960

National Coalition Against Sexual Assault: 717-232-7460

National Domestic Violence Hotline: 1-800-799-7233

National Resource Center on Domestic Violence: 1-800-537-2238

Family Violence Prevention Fund: 415-252-8900

National Organization for Victim Assistance: 202-232-6682

National Victim Center: 703-276-2880

Internet Resources

If you were raped: http://www.rainn.org/whatshould.html

Teen Rape and Abuse Resource:
   http://kidshealth.org/teen/your_mind/problems/rape_what_to_do.html

R.A.I.N.N. (Rape Abuse Incest National Network): www.rain.org

Rape Counseling (find your local resource):
   www.rainn.org/counseling.html

Rape Counseling International Resources:
   http://www.rainn.org/counseling-centers/international-
   resources.html

Men's Rape Prevention Project: http://www.mencanstoprape.org/

SOAR (Speaking Out About Rape): www.soar99.0rg

Domestic Violence Crisis: www.minot.com/~dvcc

Domestic Violence Shelter Contacts:
   http://www.dvsheltertour.org/helpusa.html

National Coalition Against Domestic Violence: www.ncadv.org

Domestic Violence Hotlines and Resources:
  www.feminist.org/911/crisis.html

International Crisis Resources (This is a world-wide directory of
  International abuse and crisis help lines.):
  http://hotpeachpages.net/a/index.html

Canada Domestic Abuse: http://www.abusehelplines.org/

International Rape and Abuse Resources:
  http://www.pandys.org/aphroditewounded/hotlines.html

Child Help USA (child abuse): www.childhelpusa.org

Self Injury (DON'T CUT) Crisis:
  http://crystal.palace.net/~llama/selfinjury/fself.html

National Suicide Prevention Lifeline:
  http://www.suicidepreventionlifeline.org/

Gay and Lesbian Information: http://www.glnh.org

Women's Health (FREE, reliable health information referrals for
  women.): http://www.4woman.gov/

Recovery (Hope Heals): http://www.hopeheals.me.uk/21.html

International Crime Victim Compensation Program Directory:
  http://www.ojp.usdoj.gov/ovc/intdir/intdir.htm

ACLU Criminal Justice Site: www.aclu.org/issues/criminal/hmcj.html

American Bar Association Network: www.abanet.org/

Anti-stalking Website: www.antistalking.com/

Dept. of Justice (Bureau of Justice Statistics): www.ojp.usdoj.gov/bjs/

Department of Justice Office for Victims of Crime:
  www.ojp.usdoj.gov/ovc/

D.O.J. (Office of Violence Against Women): www.usdoj.gov/vawo/

National Institute of Justice: www.ojp.usdoj.gov/nij/

NOVA (National Organization for Victims Assistance):
  www.try-nova.org/

Partnership Against Violence Network: www.pavnet.org/

Security On Campus: www.securityoncampus.org/

Victim Services Network: www.victimservices.org/

Suggested Reading

Date, Acquaintance, and Stranger Rape

Brownmiller, Susan. *Against Our Will*. New York: Simon and Schuster, 1975.

De Becker, Gavin. *The Gift Of Fear, and Other Survival Signals That Protect Us From Violence*. New York: Dell Publishing, 1997.

Dyer, Wayne. *Your Erroneous Zones*. Toronto, Canada: Fitzhenry and Whiteside, Ltd., 1993.

Goring, Ruth. *Date Rape*. Downers Grove, Il.: Intervarsity Press, 1996.

Landau, Elaine. *Sexual Harassment*. New York: Walker and Company, 1993.

Ledray, Linda E. *Recovering From Rape*. New York: Henry Holt and Company, 1988.

Lipman, Ira A. *How To Protect Yourself From Crime*, 3rd Edition. Chicago: Contemporary Books, 1997.

Martin, Laura. *A Life Without Fear*. Nashville: Rutledge Hill Press, 1992.

McColgan, Aileen. *The Case For Taking the Date Out of Rape*. New York: Rivers Oram Press, Division of NYU Press, 1998.

Medea, Andra and Kathleen Thompson. *Against Rape*. New York: Ferrar, Straus, Giroux, 1994.

Miller, Maryann. *Drugs and Date Rape*. Baltimore: Rosen Publishing Group, 1995.

Mufson, Susan and Rachael Krantz. *Straight Talk about Date Rape.* Checkmark Books, 1997.

Orion, Doreen. *I Know You Really Love Me: A Psychiatrist's Journal of Erotomania, Stalking, and Obsessive Love.* New York: Macmillan, 1997

Rosenberg, Marshall B., Ph.D., *Nonviolent Communication: A Language of Life.* Puddle Dancer Press: Encinitas, CA, 2003

Sanday-Reeves, Peggy. *A Woman Scorned: Acquaintance Rape on Trial.* New York: Doubleday, 1996.

Viscott, David. *I Love You, Let's Work It Out.* New York: Simon and Schuster, 1987.

Warshaw, Robin. *I Never Called It Rape.* New York: Harper and Row Publishers, 1994.

Webb, Susan. *Step Forward: Sexual Harassment and the Future of Feminism.* Lanham, Md.: Rowan and Littlefield Publishers, 1998.

Williams, Mary E. *Date Rape at Issue.* San Diego: Greenhaven Press, 1998.

Winkler, Kathleen. *Date Rape: A Hot Issue.* Springfield, N.J.: Enslow Publishers, 1999.

Wiseman, Rosalind. *Defending Ourselves: A Guide to Prevention, Self Defense and Recovery from Rape.* New York: The Noonday Press, 1994.

For Men

Beneke, Timothy. *Men on Rape: What They Have to Say about Sexual Violence.* New York: St. Martin's Press, 1983.

Funk, Rus Ervin. *Stopping Rape: A Challenge for Men.* Philadelphia: New Society Publishers, 1993.

Fossum, Merle. *Men Coming Alive in Recovery.* New York: Harper/Hazelton, 1989.

Gondolf, Edward. *Man to Man: A Guide for Men in Abusive Relationships.* New York: Sulzburger and Graham, 1994

Johnson, Scott. *Man to Man—When Your Partner Says No: Pressured Sex and Date Rape.* Brandon, Vt.: Safer Society Press, 1992.

Violence

Horsfall, Jan. *The Presence of the Past: Male Violence in the Family*. Chicago: Allen and Unwin, 1991.

Kivel, Paul. *Men's Work: How to Stop the Violence That Tears Our Lives Apart*. Center City, Mn.: Mass Market Paperback, 1992.

McKay, Matthew, Peter Rogers, and Judith McKay. *When Anger Hurts: Quieting the Storm Within*. Oakland, Ca.: New Harbinger, 1989.

Stream, Herbert, and Lucy Freeman. *Our Wish to Kill: The Murder in All Our Hearts*. New York: St. Martin's Press, 1991.

Domestic Violence

Deschner, Jeanne. *The Hitting Habit: Anger Control for Battering Couples*. New York: Free Press, 1984.

Dwight, Edgar. *I Cried; You Didn't Listen: A Survivor's Exposé of the California Youth Authority*. Venice, Ca.: Abbot, Feral House, 1991.

Gelles, Richard, and Claire Pedrick Cornell. *Intimate Violence in Families*. Phoenix: Sage, 1990.

Gelles, Richard, and Murray Strauss. *Intimate Violence*. New York: Simon and Schuster, 1988.

Gillespie, Cynthia. *Justifiable Homicide: Battered Women, Self-Defense and the Law*. Columbus, Oh.: Ohio State University Press, 1989.

Miedzian, Myriam. *Boys Will Be Boys, Breaking the Link Between Masculinity and Violence*. New York: Doubleday, 1991.

Stanko, Elizabeth. *Everyday Violence: How Women and Men Experience Sexual and Physical Danger*. Kenner, La.: Pandora, 1990

Straus, Murray, Richard Gelles, and Suzanne Steinmetz. *Behind Closed Doors: Violence in the American Family*. Waxhaw, N.C.: Anchor, 1980.

For Teens

Adams, C., and J. Fay. *Nobody Told Me It Was Rape: A Parent's Guide to Talking with Teenagers about Acquaintance Rape and Sexual Exploitation*. Santa Cruz, Ca.: Network Publications, 1984.

Bandon, Alexandra. *Date Rape*. New York: Crestwood House, 1994.

Bass, E., and Davis, L. *Beginning to Heal: A First Book For Survivors of Child Sexual Abuse.* New York: Harper, 1993.

Bean, B., and S. Bennett, S. *The Me Nobody Knows: A Recovery Guide for Teenagers.* New York: Lexington Books, 1993.

Jiivanii, Ed. *In Search of Healing.* Albuquerque, N.M.: The Survivor Press, 1993.

Parrot, Andrea. *Sexual Assault on Campus.* Lexington, Mass.: Lexington Books, 1993.

Parrot, Andrea. *Coping with Date and Acquaintance Rape.* New York: Rosen Publishing Group, 1999.

For Survivors

Maltz, W., and B. Holman. *Incest and Sexuality: A Guide to Understanding and Healing.* New York: Lexington Books, 1991.

Maltz, Wendy. *The Sexual Healing Journey: A Guide for Survivors of Sexual Abuse.* New York: HarperCollins Publishers, 1991.

Munson, L. and K. Riskin. *In Their Own Words: A Sexual Abuse Workbook for Teenage Girls.* Washington, D.C.: Child Welfare League of America, 1995.

Polese, C. *Promise Not to Tell.* New York: Beech Tree Books, 1993.

Notes

1. Bureau of Justice Statistics Special Report, "Violence Against Women," Estimates from the Redesigned Survey (U.S. Department of Justice, Office of Justice Programs, Washington DC, August 1995).
2. Herbert Koppel, "Lifetime Likelihood of Victimization" (U.S. Department of Justice, Bureau of Justice Statistics, Washington DC, 1987).
3. Robin Warshaw. *I Never Called It Rape* (New York: Harper & Row Publishers, 1988).
4. Dr. Peg Ziegler, interview by the author, Atlanta, Ga., 1989.
5. E. MacFarlane and P. Hawley, "Sexual Assault: Coping with Crisis," The Canadian Nurse (June, 1993).
6. Warshaw, *I Never Called It Rape*.
7. Illinois Coalition Against Sexual Assault. "Acquaintance Rape Sexual Violence: Facts and Statistics" (Springfield, Il., 1994).
8. Warshaw, *I Never Called It Rape*.
9. Lawrence A. Greenfield, "Sex Offenses and Offenders—An Analysis of Data on Rape and Sexual Assault" (U.S. Department of Justice, Office of Justice Programs, Washington DC, February 1997).
10. The Community Epidemiology Work Group, "Epidemiologic Trends in Drug Abuse Advance Report," National Institute on Drug Abuse (June 1995).

11. Coalition Against Sexual Assault. "Acquaintance Rape Sexual Violence: Facts and Statistics" (Springfield, Il., 1994)

12. N.M. Malamuth, "Rape Proclivity Among Males," Social Issues (January 1981).

13. Greenfield, Sex Offenses and Offenders-An Analysis of Data on Rape and Sexual Assault.

14. Janet Bode, *Fighting Back—How To Cope With The Medical, Emotional, and Legal Consequences of Rape* (New York: MacMillan, 1978).

15. Karen S. Peterson, "Full Disclosure," *USA Today* (16 December 1994).

16. Peterson, "Full Disclosure."

17. Gordon Clay, The National Men's Resource Calendar (Vol. 9, No. 1, 1993).

18. Patricia Tjaden and Nancy Thoennes, "Stalking in America: Findings From the National Violence Against Women Surve" (U.S. Department of Justice, National Institute of Justice, Washington DC, 1998).

19. Louis Harris and Associates, Inc., "First Comprehensive National Survey of American Women Finds Them at Significant Risk," (The Commonwealth Fund, New York, 14 July 1993).

20. "The Many Faces of Domestic Violence and It's Impact on the Workplace," Savvy Management (New York: The Body Shop, 1998).

Index

D

Damages, monetary, 109, 117, 145

Damage to victim, 31

Danger spots, 37–41

Date as game or battle, 73–74

Date rape, 9

Date Rape Triangle, 33–36

Dating violence, 169–173

De Becker, Gavin, 16–18, 67

Defense mechanisms, 50

Delaware, University of, 40

Delays, 36, 144

Demands, 205

Denial

confusion and, 46

family's, 124–125, 133–134

rapist's, 1–2, 29, 66, 74, 81

responsibility, of, 195–196

victim's, 25–26, 64, 89, 127, 130, 174

Dependence, 124, 169–170

Depression, 123, 126, 133

Detachment, 125

Details, too many, 67–68

Diet, 129

Disbelief, 120, 121–122, 133

Discrimination, 71–72, 139

Disorientation. See Confusion

Dissing, 201

Dissociative states, 54

Distress, 125

District Attorneys, 117

Documentation, 143–144, 157, 165–168

DOJ (Drug Enforcement Administration), 56

Domestic violence, 151, 169, 173–176

Doom, feeling of, 25. See also Inner guidance

Double standard, 5, 44

Dread, feeling of, 25. See also Inner guidance

Dreams, 125

Drinking. See Alcohol

Drug Enforcement Administration (DOJ), 56

Drug-facilitated sexual assault, 51

Drugs

communication and, 77, 80

effects of, 52–53

excuse, as, 171

gang rape and, 69

legality of, 54

overview, 51

reporting, 115

resources about, 56–57

testing for, 55–56, 113

Dry Rush, 40

Dulled senses, 45–46. See also Confusion

Dysfunction, 202

E

Economic dependence, 169–170

Education, 65–66

Effects of rape, 30–31, 65

Electricity, 97–100

Electro-muscular disruption

(EMD), 98–100

E-mail, 164–165

Embarrassment, 120, 122

EMD (electro-muscular disruption), 98–100

Emotions, 75, 126, 129–130. See also Feelings

Empathy, 205–206

Employment Law Center (Worker's Rights Clinics), 146

Equal Employment Opportunity Commission, 139, 146

Equality, 21–22, 71–72, 180–181

Equal Rights Advocates, 146

Escape, 25, 26, 59, 88

Estrich, Susan, 89

Ethics, 44

Evidence, 55–56, 110–114, 117. See also Documentation

Exaggeration, 199

Expectations about victim, 124–125

Eyeball push, 87

Eye contact, 84

F

Fabrication, 50, 180, 184–185

Facebook, 166

Factors in rape, 62, 64–65

Familiarity, 15

Families, 115, 121, 124–125, 132–135

Fantasies, 29, 49, 122–123, 149

"Fatal Attraction" cases, 150

Fault. See Blame

FBI, 166, 167

Fear, 9, 18, 123, 125

Feelings. See also Attitudes toward women; Emotions; specific feelings

    expressing, 200

    family's, 134

    hurt, 201–202

    identifying, 199–200, 205–206

    victim's, 31, 55

Fighting back, 28, 43, 86–90. See also Resistance; Weapons

Figures. See Statistics

Films, 49

Financial assistance, 114

"Finger" Ultimate Directory, 164

Five-Star Program, 40

Flashbacks, 125

Flunitrazepam (Rohypnol), 51, 52–53, 54

Food and Drug Administration, 56

Force

    acquaintance rape, in, 88

    emotional, 28

    evidence of, 112–113

    factors in, 77

    myths about, 49–50

    threats of, 9

    vague, 196

Forced teaming, 67

Forgiveness, 125

Fraternity men, 37–40, 69

Freedom, 197

Friends, 124, 132–135

I Never Called it Rape (Warshaw), 61, 73

Inhibitions, 23, 44

Injuries, 126

Inner guidance, 18, 25, 64, 89, 101

Instincts, 36, 45, 66, 84

Internet, 31, 161–168, 208–209

Internet Relay Chat (IRC), 165–166

Intimacy, 15, 76

Intimidation, 22, 28, 109, 113

Intoxication. See Alcohol

Intuition, 18, 103

IRC (Internet Relay Chat), 165–166

Irritability, 125

Isolation
    aftermath, in, 127, 133
    consequence, as, 31
    factor in rapes, as, 16, 24, 33
    groups, in, 41

J

Jealousy, 151, 170

Johnke, Erik, 73

Judgments, moralistic, 194–195, 198–199, 203

Jurisdiction, 114

Justice system, 107

K

Ketamine hydrochloride (Ketamine), 51, 53–54

Knives, 93

Krishnamurti, J., 199

L

Language, 194. See also Communication

La Rocha (flunitrazepam), 52–53

Law enforcement, 47–48

Ledray, R.N., Ph.D., Linda E., 110, 121

Legal process, 114–117

Legal profession, 48

Letterman, David, 149

Liquid Exstasy, 52

Listening, 205–206

"Little Sisters," 38

Locations of rapes, 37–41, 59

Locker-room talk, 73

Los Angeles Commission on Assaults Against Women, 110

Love, 62, 76, 83, 170, 188, 189–190

Love Obsession Stalker, 149–150

Lovers, 123

Lying, 67–68

M

Mace (CS or CN Tear Gas), 93–94

Manhood, 69, 73

Manipulation, 67, 68

Marijuana, 50

Marriage, 50

Martial arts, 101–103

Mature women, 14–15

Media, 49, 60, 62

Medical exams, 110–114

Memory, 122

Men are from Mars (Gray), 72

Men Can Stop Rape, 56

P

Pain thresholds, 95, 96
Panic, 125
Parents, 167–168, 172–173
Parties, 36
Patience, 134–135
PCP, 52, 54
Peacemaking, 191–192
Peer pressure, 45
Penalties, legal, 50
Pepper scale, 95
Pepper spray (Oleoresin
    Capsicum), 94–97
Perceptions of women, 44
Perfect gentleman, 10, 19–20
Personalities of rapists, 59–66
Personality of victim, 59
Phone calls, 159–161
Physical abuse, 9, 86
Physical harassment, 140
Physical maneuvers, 86–88
Physical responses, 124
Plans. See also Prevention
    rapist's, 33, 63–64, 66, 71
    stalking victim's, 157–158
    victim's, 34–36, 96, 172–173
Police reports
    fabricated, 50, 180, 184–185
    importance of, 97, 113–114,
    157
    likeliness of, 107
    procedures for, 110–116
    reasons for, 108–109, 128
    stalking, of, 155
    use as threat, 29–30

Popularity, 170
Post-Traumatic Stress Disorder
    (PTSD), 125–126
Power. See also Control
    abuser's, 187
    goal, as, 68
    harassment and, 142
    motivator, as, 11, 15, 64, 66, 76
    stranger rape, in, 67
    victim's, 80, 122, 129, 197
Power Assertive Rapist, 62–63
Power reassurance, 61–62
Power Reassurance Rapist, 29
Precautions, 34–36, 55, 71. See also
    Prevention
Precinct, 114
Preconceptions, 46–47
Preparations, 34–36
Prevention. See also Precautions;
    Protection
    case study, in, 20–30
    communication and, 74
    criminal techniques and,
    67–69
    danger spots, of, 41
    disrespect for women and, 21
    personality types, for, 62–65
    phrases for, 81–82
    police, by, 109
    social attitudes and, 76
    techniques, 34–36
    weapons, with, 97–98
Privacy, 161–168
Privacy manager, 161
Professional help, 134–135

Progesterex, 56

Promiscuity, 124

Proof, 117

Prosecutions, 47–48, 109, 110, 164–168

Prosecutors, 116, 117

Protection, 175–176. See also Prevention

Protective orders, 156–157

Proving oneself, 68

PTSD (Post-Traumatic Stress Disorder), 125–126

Put-downs, 200–202

Q

Quid pro quo, 139

R

R2, 52–53

Rage, 65, 69, 122, 203

Rape
actions after, 55–56
characterization of, 9, 81, 83, 129, 183–184
effects of, 65
factors in, 23, 50, 51
locations of, 37–41
perceptions of, 9–10, 49, 60, 62

Rape, Abuse, and Incest National Network, 57

Rape crisis centers, 108, 110

Rapists
attitudes toward women of, 28–29, 62
attraction to, 64
identity of, 10, 15, 26, 46–47
motivations of, 60
personalities of, 59–65

Real Rape (Estrich), 89

Recovering from Rape (Ledray), 121

Recovery. See Healing process; Help; Support

Rehearsing, 34–35

Rejection, 204

Relationships
approaches to, 20
attitudes toward, 76–78
communication and, 79–80
conceptions of, 61, 74
enhancing, 201–202
healthy, 46, 173, 188, 203
rapist, with, 121
victim's, 119, 132–135

Relaxation, 129

Reliving event, 126

Reports, 145–146. See also Police reports

Requests, 204–205

Resistance, 22–23, 28, 62, 63. See also Fighting back; Weapons

Resources, 109, 207–209
healing, for, 31

Responses to rape, 4–5, 66, 120–126, 121, 124

Responsibility
arousal, for, 11
behavior, for, 20–21
denial of, 195–196
feelings, for, 199

police reports, with, 114–115
resources, 31, 90
strategies, 129
techniques, 132–135
trials, with, 117
Surviving Sexual Assault (Ledray), 110
Symptoms, 30–31, 120–126

T

Talk. See Communication
Talk therapy, 133
Tannen, Deborah, 72
Tasers, 98–100
Tear Gas (Mace), 93–94
Teasing, 20–21. See also Arousal
Techniques, criminal, 67–69
Teens, 170–173
Telephone calls, 159–161
Telephones, 36
Testicals, 87
Thoughts
    cause, as, 183, 187, 199
    lack of, 202
    language and, 195–196
    obsessive, 182
    responses and, 197
    victim's, 127
Threats, 9, 27
Thrill as motivator, 63
Time, 133
Time off, 127
Title VII (Civil Rights Act of 1964), 139
Tone of voice, 78, 84

Trauma, 30–31, 90
Trials, 117
Triangle, date rape, 33–36
Triggers, 124, 199
Trophies, 63
Trust
    employee's, 142
    loss of, 19, 123
    rapist, in, 16–17, 64
    victim's, 30, 31, 65, 130
Typecasting, 68

U

Universities, 40, 145–146
USA Today, 141

V

Vague forces, 196
Venereal disease, 110, 127
Verbal harassment, 140
Verbal self-defense, 83–86
Victims, 34, 46–47, 90
Violence
    factors in, 23, 44
    media, in, 62
    personalities and, 62, 63
    rape, in, 67, 69, 86
    relationships, in, 188
    stalkers, of, 151
    threats of, 9, 28, 61
    thrill, as, 65
Viscott, Dr. David, 77
Visual harassment, 140
Visual messages, 79
Vulnerability, 14–18, 64, 71, 76

About the Author

Scott Lindquist is certified through the Florida State Attorney General's Office as a crime prevention practitioner and through the Georgia Crime Prevention Association as a crime prevention specialist in rape prevention. He is a graduate of the Florida Crime Prevention Training Institute.

Lindquist has presented his crime prevention seminar to hundreds of thousands of people in universities such as Southern Connecticut State University, Georgia Tech University, and the City University of New York, as well as in corporations such as AT&T, 3M Corp., American Express, and Texaco, and to government agencies such as the Internal Revenue Service, the Social Security Administration, and the U.S. Federal Reserve Bank. He also has been interviewed on hundreds of television and radio stations worldwide. He has appeared in articles in *Cosmopolitan* (both United States and United Kingdom) and in *Australian* Magazine.

Scott Lindquist has made it his life's work to eradicate rape as an issue for American women. He is available to speak to college, university, or corporate groups, and he can be reached at:

201 Parkaire Crossing
Marietta, Georgia 30007-1452
Phone: 770-973-1440, Cell: 678-923-4898
Email: scottlindquist4375@yahoo.com